PEOPLE HAVE MORE FUN THAN ANYBODY

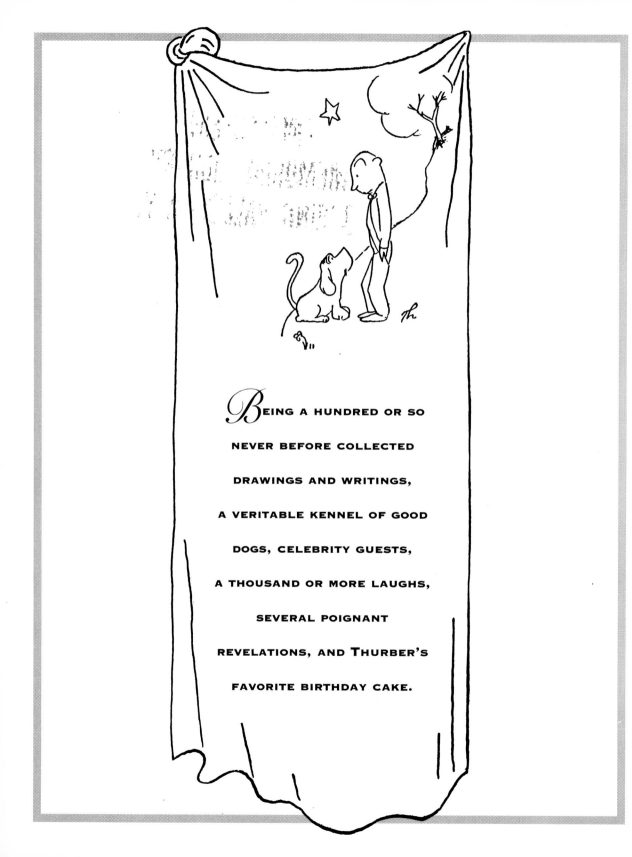

BEING A HUNDRED OR SO
NEVER BEFORE COLLECTED
DRAWINGS AND WRITINGS,
A VERITABLE KENNEL OF GOOD
DOGS, CELEBRITY GUESTS,
A THOUSAND OR MORE LAUGHS,
SEVERAL POIGNANT
REVELATIONS, AND THURBER'S
FAVORITE BIRTHDAY CAKE.

PEOPLE HAVE MORE FUN THAN ANYBODY

A Centennial Celebration of

Drawings and Writings by

JAMES THURBER

EDITED BY MICHAEL J. ROSEN

HARCOURT BRACE & COMPANY

NEW YORK   SAN DIEGO   LONDON

Requests for permission to make copies of any
part of the work should be mailed to: Permissions Department.
Harcourt Brace & Company, 6277 Sea Harbor Drive,
Orlando, Florida 32887-6777.

Grateful acknowledgment is made to The New Yorker, where
most of these drawings and writings first appeared.

Acknowledgments for previously published material appear
under "Sources" at the end of this book.

Library of Congress Cataloging-in-Publication Data
Thurber, James, 1894–1961.
People have more fun than anybody: a centennial celebration of
drawings and writings by James Thurber: being a hundred or so . . . /edited by
Michael J. Rosen.—1st ed.
p.   cm.
0-15-100094-8
I. Rosen, Michael J., 1954– . II. Title.
PS3539.H94A6   1994b
818'.5209—dc20   93-37922

Designed by Joy Chu
Printed in the United States of America
First edition
A B C D E

ACKNOWLEDGMENTS

THE EDITOR WOULD LIKE TO EXTEND HIS ONGOING gratitude to Rosemary Thurber, James's daughter, and a newer version of this appreciation to Sara Thurber Sauers, James's granddaughter, for their generous opinions and enthusiasm regarding this and the other projects involving Thurber's work. Thanks, too, continue in the direction of The Thurber House—to my colleagues there and to the many volunteers who make most of the days there something of a celebration.

Contents

James Thurber

JAMES THURBER

℘REFACE

A FEW YEARS AGO, I DEPARTED FROM THE THURBER Country of Columbus, Ohio, where I act as literary director of the writer's center in Thurber's boyhood home, and spent some time with my brother in the other Thurber Country of West Cornwall, Connecticut, where Thurber lived from 1945 until his death in 1961. It's an unassuming town near Kent and Litchfield, having, in Thurber's day, little more than a general store. The town has hardly enlarged. There are still more deer than people, according to the locals who grow rhododendrons (a favorite food of deer). In fact my brother and I couldn't find a gas station—an open one—anywhere. As the needle continued to drop on the gas gauge of my brother's Fiat Spider, so did his confidence in the miracle of the gas tank. Ours was not to be a modern-day Chanukah story: The little fuel would not last us eight days or even eight miles.

When a state trooper found us marooned in the parking lot of a closed gas station, he offered the fact that the station would open at 7:00 A.M. and that we "might as well get comfy" in the obviously uncomfy car. When that didn't get a laugh, he suggested, "Well, then, you better pray some deer will come along and haul you outa here—there's nothing else in these parts." Finally, having run through his repertoire, he offered us two gallons of gasoline from a nearby highway-patrol pump. And, what's more, he insisted that they were free. I declared this a Thurberesque moment—one that might easily take its place in the litany of aggravations Thurber compiled in works such as "I Break Everything I Touch."

Thurber's house in West Cornwall is a stately fourteen-room Colonial structure that resembles a hand-painted Christmas ornament or a boxy inn from a fancy train set. This is the place of hilarity and high spirits, hospitality and recoveries from hospital stays. This is the house featured in Thurber's later monologues and diatribes, though his blindness kept him from ever really seeing it. This is the house that his second wife, Helen, maintained in an unvarying arrangement, so that Jim could move about with the ease of a sighted person. And here is where Thurber made his last heroic attempts at drawing, argued with Samuel Goldwyn over the sale of "The Secret Life of Walter Mitty," and wrote the last twelve of his thirty-one—now thirty-two—books.

Living in a dense grove of cathedral pines beside Mohawk State Forest, Thurber could hear and smell his towering evergreen neighbors. He often wrote of sensing their height and grandeur. But as we approached the area, we saw an expanse of jagged tree trunks—dead? burned?—poking through lush ground cover, with a few lone evergreens scattered here and there, whose girth indicated that these very trees had featured in Thurber's memory. Nearing Thurber's corner, we noticed another wide embankment of dead, gray trees, broken timbers, leafless limbs. A conflagration? And there, amid a few saplings and bare ornamentals, inside a white wooden fence lined with modest shrubs, stood Thurber's neat white house, with its black shutters. As for the legendary cathedral pines, all but a few less than stately exceptions had disappeared. Later, we were told that a tornado had devastated the area just months before.

That particular West Cornwall home was spared. It hasn't become a national treasure, like the house here at 77 Jefferson Avenue in Columbus, but the dwelling *is* occupied by people who treasure Thurber's legacy: the actor Sam Waterston and his family. While I've admired Waterston in many films, I've never forgotten his early performance as the ingenuous

Midwesterner Nick Carroway in the film adaptation of *The Great Gatsby* —"one of the bright American jewels on anybody's shelf," Thurber said of this, his favorite book. So I've also imagined, with Thurber's presiding guidance, that it was Jay Gatsby who lived and died in that house in West Cornwall and that Nick Carroway has taken up residence there, tending the warmth and light of its memory.

Thurber's restored Columbus home, where he lived from 1913 through 1917, inspired many of the stories in *My Life and Hard Times*. Although our electricity doesn't leak, as Thurber's mother claimed, resident writers are often asked if they have sighted the ghost on the back stairs. Alarms are heard in the night, although most often this happens when a squirrel chews through the fire-alarm wires and the security system misfires. It seems appropriate to bestow on Thurber's work the permanence that his mythologized Columbus home has received—particularly that less available work that Thurber himself never retrieved from magazines and newspapers. *People Have More Fun Than Anybody* presents a celebratory sampling of Thurber's uncollected humor. This is quite literally a restoration: the re-presenting of a neglected part of Thurber's canon, a part that has fallen, just as the house had, into desuetude.

The preferred term for the sort of historically sensitive restoration we undertook on The Thurber House is "preservation"; we were required to maintain all extant structures and original artifacts rather than to replace worn or weathered materials with reproductions. To continue the comparison then, this centennial collection is a preservation of words and drawings that previously inhabited only the crumbling pages of early *New Yorkers* and defunct magazines like *PM*—pages crumbling like the plaster ceilings or the oak planks of a late-nineteenth-century house. But instead of rewiring, skim-coating, refinishing, fund-raising, and agonizing over zoning ordinances, this job required squinting at microfiche, interlibrary loaning, annotating, culling, and the shameless pestering of reference librarians. The truth is, Thurber's work needed almost nothing in the way of reconditioning for its new habitation. (Notably more troubling was my own ignorance of midcentury cultural history: I have gathered a bouquet of incredulous exclamation points from the people I queried about certain of Thurber's allusions: "You don't remember Arnold Rothstein? Or Lowell Thomas's voice? What! You've never even *heard* of Stoopnagle and Budd!")

Each time I read among Thurber's uncollected works, I find abidingly clear, plainspoken, and yet unpredictable sentences—classical composition but also classically Thurber. It continually surprises me that although I do find pieces about figures or phenomena I cannot bring to mind—tennis stars from sixty years ago, parodies of magazines that haven't appeared in decades, profiles (entitled "Where Are They Now?") featuring people who had already dropped out of sight in the 1930s— the majority of the work offers little impediment to a contemporary reader. What's even more remarkable about this is that Thurber's are primarily works that pivot on humor, which, it can be argued, bears least well the shifting connotations of politics, the fading of popular personalities, and the vicissitudes of morality.

Time's cover story on James Thurber (July 9, 1951) quotes T. S. Eliot detecting—or predicting—Thurber's singular longevity:

> It [Thurber's work] is a form of humor which is also a way of saying something serious. There is a criticism of life at the bottom of it. It is serious and even somber. Unlike so much humor, it is not merely a criticism of manners—that is, of the superficial aspects of society at a given moment—but something more profound. His writings and also his illustrations are capable of surviving the immediate environment and time out of which they spring.

Several elements combine to create this vitality. First of all, Thurber did not retreat from the ephemeral stuff of everyday life, yet he tended to treat it with a broad reflection and a chronological overview that didn't, with three swipes of invective, eliminate the subject once and for all. He typically considered a topic as an evolving genus rather than a wayward species, allowing his readers the chance to tease out the fundamental repercussions and philosophical possibilities within each. Although Thurber pulled few punches when he took on such calamities as the ignorance of youth, the abuse of the English language, or the terrorist tactics of the

House Un-American Activities Committee, most of Thurber's writing shows the restraint of a confident talent that allows each reader to participate in and complement the humor by recalling a common reference or individual memory.

Thurber's humor still prods and chides because of this refusal to deflate a subject into absurd simplicity. Thurber himself echoed T. S. Eliot's remark about the humorist's ambivalent—or, perhaps better, ambidextrous—bent. He told the *Time* reporter, "The human species is both horrible and wonderful. Occasionally, I get very mad at human beings, but there's nothing you can do about it. I like people and hate them at the same time. I wouldn't draw them in cartoons, if I didn't think they were horrible; and I wouldn't write about them, if I didn't think they were wonderful." If his works had issued from a single tirade of emotion, their arguments would have possessed a much briefer shelf life.

Moreover, the prose itself confers a patina of posterity on each piece collected here. In interviews, Thurber often called himself a rewriter, rather than a writer. His sentences are rarely dated by stylistic quirks, fashionable penchants, and gratuitous conventions. Many of his works protest against or warn of such things as *TYPOGRAPHICAL ELEPHANTIASIS!!!* (Q.E.D.) and the cavalier use of jargon. Russell Baker recently called Thurber's pieces "jewels of English writing," adding, "Maybe what America needs at this critical time when everybody is bloating the language with dead ballast like 'at this critical time' is more reading material that was written at the rate of eight hundred words per fortnight." Thurber's writing style is foremost that of a journalist assessing and interpreting facts as he sees them: *I have intercepted some news, and I feel it's my duty to explain it to you, or at least to document it for us and for all time.* His approach, rather than that of the authority, was often that of fellow witness, remarking on this occurrence, that trend, some phenomenon. His forms of disquisition include frank bafflement, mischief-making juxtaposition, gleeful indignation, feigned investigation, incredulous curiosity, schoolmarmish upbraiding, impeccable parody, and justifiable outrage—whatever pinned the matter to the mat.

Often Thurber views a subject from a layman's vantage. An early series of articles for *The Magazine of Business* begins:

> I know less about finance and business—and that goes for commerce and industry too—than almost anyone else in the world. Hence I can approach these subjects with a new and, I trust, refreshing viewpoint. Sometimes I think the best critic is the layman. That is why editors and publishers often give manuscripts to the stenographer or the charwoman to read. In their criticism these fresh minds often suggest valuable revolutionary ideas, such as tearing the manuscripts up and beginning over again.

Reading *People Have More Fun Than Anybody*, you will hear Thurber on the subject of pedigreed dogs, homing pigeons, Mary Pickford, polo ponies, Eleanor Roosevelt, polar bears, Martians, postal sweepstakes, mechanization, marriage, bicycles, Admiral Byrd, Mr. Big, and the billions of U.S. dollars out of circulation and hidden between mattresses. In other words, you will find Thurber at large and getting larger in his favorite role of the natural raconteur who assumes very little knowledge on the part of his listener/reader and who agreeably takes pains to explain with clear yet conversational concision. His tone has all the necessary modesty needed to forgive those few lapses into pride and self-righteousness. Consider this passage from a column in the *Bermudian* entitled "The Old Year." Here is that cagey blend of horror and humor to which Eliot alluded; serious clarity tempered with Thurber's inimitable musing:

> It was quite a year, 1951, full of disturbing signs and curious portents and nobody in his right mind would want to live through it again. Strange green lights began appearing in the southwest skies; hunters, possibly affected by the lights, took to shooting does and fawns; mothers, making the beds of basketball players, home from college, discovered as much as $5000 in currency hidden in the mattresses; little girls rifled shoe boxes containing the life's savings of doctors who didn't trust the banks, but trusted little girls; owners of diamonds and emeralds, who didn't trust hotel safes, left $3,000,000

worth of jewels in their hotel rooms, where thieves could find them in the dark; female secretaries came to work wearing platinum mink furs worth $7500; a cocker spaniel, belonging to a Des Moines dentist, brought a wallet home one evening containing $4308. He said he had won the money betting on a fixed dogfight. A search of my own French poodle's secret hiding places, I am glad to say, reveals that she hasn't got any money at all.

The few Americans who hadn't suspected one another before began to suspect one another of suspecting them.

As for his drawings—with the exception of those few that mention a popular figure of the day, such as FDR's granddaughter Sistie Dall, or the tennis celebrity Henri Cochet—they remain characterizations of a clearly identifiable social creature, the human being. This book brings together over seventy cartoons, and while some depict behaviors that may be sillier than those we'd like to claim for guests at our own homes, they all suggest a traditional grouping we're sure to recognize, despite the reupholstering of idioms. When Thurber's *Men, Women and Dogs* appeared fifty years ago, W. Somerset Maugham wrote to the author about this "grand" book. "It's the perfect book," he said, "to turn over while one is drinking a cocktail. The only thing against it is that it makes a cocktail seem rather wan & pale." While paging through the cartoons here, you might try Maugham's comparison yourself. Alternately, you might reassess the German Expressionist George Grosz's opinion of the cartoons, which he set down in a fan letter to Thurber:

They once told me, when old man Matisse came down to New York to collect a huge fee from old sourpuss Barnes for a so called mural he did for him (on canvas) . . . reporters asked him who he thought was the best draftsman in USA. As the story goes . . . Henri answered: the only good artist you have in New York is a man named Thurber . . . and that goes for me too.

Finally, a more personal note. Am I alone in thinking that many of today's "current affairs" and "exposés" and "front-line" reports cry out for Thurber—or, at least, a Thurberesque essay? I'd hazard that those of us who have relished Thurber's memorable work are partly equipped with all manner of wariness and curiosity and skepticism supplied by this writer's various guises. Perhaps what we mean by Thurber's literary immortality is not only that his works possess an intrinsic vitality but also that they continue to offer themselves as models of perception and communication for future readers. So in place of *his* voice, continuing its commentary, we have the chance to absorb the examples he offers and adapt them to our own assessments of this life and hard times.

Sixty years ago, give or take a few weeks, Thurber reconsidered Admiral Byrd's discovery of yet another part of the Antarctic. His less than celebratory piece, "More Ice Added to U.S. As Thousands Cheer," offers this salutary perspective: "You can fly right over something without discovering it, discover something farther on, and then come back and discover what, if you had been on dog sledges, you would have been bound to discover first." I hope that this collection is not only a preservation but a coming-back-on-a-dog-sledge to find Thurber on the occasion of the hundredth anniversary of his birth on December 8, 1894. Aside from being the perfect Thurber conveyance, the dog sledge offers itself as a reasonable metaphor for his deliberate style of writing; it is also relatively manageable for a mechanically disinclined dog person.

Helen Thurber often said that when her husband threw a party, it always hit someone. Well, here's your chance to join the party. Your small part in this hundredth-birthday celebration is to turn to page 159 and whip up Jim's favorite cake. Once it's frosted and ready to serve, pour yourself and a friend some coffee (you'll want someone nearby to whom you can read aloud the funniest paragraphs), and cut two thick slices. Oh, and if there's a dog nearby, call him or her over just for the swell solidarity of it all. (No chocolate for dogs, of course. It's worse for them than it is for you.) Now you're all set to open this new present of yours, settle in for the duration, and have more fun than anybody.

Go Away, You Look Human!

MEN, WOMEN, AND DOGS

I DIDN'T REALLY GET INTO THE SPIRIT OF THE NEW magazine called *Bachelor* until I reached page 64 of Volume I, Number 1. On that page Baron Giorgio Suriani, organizer and president of the Noblemen's Club of New York, a gentleman who we are told is uncommonly sincere and sensitive, has an article gallantly entitled "The Insolence of American Women." American women, it comes out, have an abrupt way of breaking off a conversation with the Baron and walking away. He doesn't know why they do that and he seems to think that all American women do it to everybody. Maybe I can give the Baron a hint or two as to what is the trouble in his case. He writes, in one place: "One trait which we are prone to call insolence is the habit the modern American woman has of what I might term 'putting on the airs.' " Now, no matter what you may think, Baron, there is no such term as "putting on the airs." Very likely some American woman has abruptly walked away from you when you used that expression, in order to turn on the heat, believing that you were trying to say you were cold. "Putting on airs" is what you mean. Incidentally, should you actually be cold in one of our drawing rooms, I would not advise you to ask your hostess to "turn on the heat"

because then she might, as we say, "let you have it" or "give it to you." "The heat," in this sense, is the same as "the works," and you should be happy that the ladies have not given to you this works but have instead walked away and left you to be the alone. I think it is quite clear that American women walk away from you during a conversation because they do not understand what you are talking about. You say, for instance, "It is one of the most annoying things I have ever known to have the most fascinating woman assume a vague stare while a man is talking, and without apology suddenly interrupt by murmuring an appointment excuse and hastily bidding goodby." Phrases like "an appointment excuse" give what I might term a betray to the fact that not always you perhaps have given an expression of the clear, if you come after what I mean. As one uncommonly sincere and sensitive gentleman to another, how in the hell can a woman go on with a conversation into which of a constantly is occurring this phraseology kind?

Before I leave you abruptly with an appointment excuse, let us examine just one more sentence of yours: "It is not without the boundary of the gods that even a man with a title may awaken in the morning with a beating headache." "Beating" is pretty close, and I rather like it, although it might be hard to pick up in a quick conversation, but "the boundary of the gods" is very far away from "the realm of possibility," which you apparently were trying to get at. "The boundary of the gods" can mean, if it means anything, only that mythical region called Olympus. Hence what you say in the sentence I have quoted is: "It is not without Olympus that even a man with a title may awaken in the morning with a beating headache." May I say that it is not without the boundary of the gods that someday you will meet an American woman who, in execrable Italian, will ask after the health of your great Premier, calling him Il Ducky? I wonder whether you will carry on—or walk abruptly away?

In passing on to my favorite article in *Bachelor*—and possibly in the whole range of American belles-lettres—let us visit page 72 just long enough to quote one sentence from Mr. Lucius Beebe. He writes: "The symbols of success and achievement in the world are still tailcoats, footmen, and the slightly unsteady footwork deriving from having carelessly consumed a double bottle of Perrier-Jouet during dinner." I thought you would want to know what the symbols of success and achievement in the world still are. Now we turn back three pages to my favorite article, a piece called "Dogs Have Their Place," by Mr. Freeman Lloyd. Mr. Lloyd's use of English is so extraordinary as to make Baron Suriani out to be, by comparison, a meticulous, impeccable, and stuffy old purist. As for dogs, Mr. Lloyd thinks far less of an unpedigreed dog than Baron Suriani thinks of an American woman or than Mr. Beebe thinks of a sober man without a tailcoat and a footman. We'll gradually come to that. Let us begin at the beginning, where Mr. Lloyd starts off with all the ease and grace of a 1902 Cadillac going up a hill.

"Do you know," he asks, "that a man may be known by the breed of dog he affects, has as a companion or for the purposes of his game-hunting inclinations? Yet such is the case; indeed, a wrong dog in the wrong place sort of gives the man away." You might think that Mr. Lloyd's literary style couldn't get worse, but it does. A few lines farther on he writes: "Such dogs as these will not only guard your home, but their very appearances shall make hoboes and other undesirables keep away from your premises." The only explanation I can give for Mr. Lloyd's shift from "will" to "shall" here is that he thinks "shall" is pretty chi-chi and ought to be stuck in now and then for tone. Later on in his piece he uses the *soigné* future tense again. Mr. Lloyd just cannot abide tenses or dogs that do not seem chic to him. He tells about a monstrously deplorable man and dog who were to be observed walking boldly on Madison Avenue one day. "The unfortunate canine creature was a smooth fox terrier not of blue-book parentage," writes Mr. Lloyd. "The fool of a fellow was making his dog carry in its mouth one of those five-and-ten-cent store rubber rats. At the same time he was making a fool of himself, the dog, and mayhap a few of the public. And so this hobbledehoy strutted along. . . . Here was an example of the milksop man as the thing paraded on a Gotham thoroughfare. Here was a characterization that might suit my friends of the stage and screen." I submit this, without analysis, as one of the most remarkable paragraphs of our time.

Before we go on to a further examination of Mr. Lloyd's philosophy of men and dogs, it may be interesting to inspect a certain English usage of which he is extremely fond. This is the linking of synonyms with "or." He writes: "Very large dogs are not suitable for the often limited space or room for dogs in an apartment." After that come: "rough or rough-coated dogs," "personal or private hunting trips," "shade or color of reeds," "cover or hide in which the shooter waits," "decoys or sham ducks," and "do not halt or stay in your choice." I cannot think or imagine how our writer or author got into this mess or mixup and can only wonder or speculate as to why or how come the editors or publishers allowed it to appear or be printed. Certainly it must not go on or continue.

Mr. Lloyd's tribute to gun dogs I am sure you will enjoy. He writes: "These are the dogs that make robust men out of weaklings—strong, husky, athletic, life-enjoying lads fond of observing Mother Nature at her fullest and best, imbued as they are with present and future thoughts of hunting." I can't decide which would be harder: for a person to be imbued with a future thought or for a gun dog to make a robust man out of a weakling. In taking his leave of gun dogs and their owners, Mr. Lloyd has this thought to give us: "The name of a first-class game-shot becomes a household word."

Let us now go on to Mr. Freeman Lloyd's deathless explanation of why you should be possessed of, as he puts it, a pedigreed dog instead of one that isn't pedigreed. "Should you have to move where your dog will not be welcome," he says, "and you wish to sell him, the pedigreeless dog will be next to valueless either to give away or to breed from. So do not let anyone pass off to you a pedigreeless puppy or older dog—that is if you wish to be possessed of a dog that shall be worth your care and attention." (There's that fancy "shall" again!) Mr. Lloyd's closing revelation of a sight that distresses him marks the high point of his message. "Candidly," he writes, "I don't like to meet a smart man or an attractive woman when he or she is attended by a half-bred dog. The sight appears to be unseemly. It might be a sign that the person has no understanding friends even to hint that a mongrel as an up-to-date individual's companion is quite as noticeable as are dirty shoes or a hole in milady's stocking." Honest to God.

"*Go away, you look human!*"

"You don't understand. The mascot isn't supposed to participate in the game."

𝓘 LIKE DOGS

I AM NOT A DOG LOVER. A DOG LOVER TO ME MEANS A DOG that is in love with another dog. I am a great admirer of certain dogs, just as I am an admirer of certain men, and I dislike certain dogs as much as I dislike certain men. Mr. Stanley Walker in his attack on dogs brought out the very sound contention that too much sentimental gush has been said and written about man's love for the dog and the dog's love for man. (This gush, I should say, amounts to about one ten-thousandth of the gush that has been printed and recited about man's love for woman, and vice versa, since Shelley wrote "O, lift me from the grass! I die, I faint, I fail! Let thy love in kisses rain on my lips and eyelids pale.") It is significant that none of the gush about dogs has been said or written by

Editor's Note: Texas-born Stanley Walker, 1898–1962, worked as a newspaper man for most of his life. He wrote several books, including *The Night Club Era*, *Mrs. Astor's Horse*, and a biography of Thomas E. Dewey.

dogs. I once showed a copy of Senator Vest's oration to one of my dogs and he sniffed at it and walked away. No dog has ever gone around quoting any part of it. We see, then, that this first indictment of dogs— that they have called forth so much sentimental woofumpoofum—is purely and simply an indictment of men. I think we will find this to be true of most of Mr. Walker's indictments against the canine world: he takes a swing at dogs and socks men and women in the eye.

Mr. Walker began his onslaught with a one-sided and prejudiced account of how a *little* red chow *on a leash* (the italics are mine) pulled a knife on Mr. Gene Fowler, a large red man who has never been on a leash in his life. Neither the dog nor the woman who was leading the dog are quoted; we don't get their side of the brawl at all. The knife was not even examined for paw prints. Nobody proved anything. There isn't a judge in the world who wouldn't have thrown the case out of court, probably with a sharp reprimand for Mr. Fowler. So far, then, Mr. Walker hasn't got a leg to stand on.

The next crack that Mr. Walker makes is to the effect that the dog is "cousin to the wolf." (He doesn't even say what wolf.) Now, the dog is no more cousin to the wolf than I am niece to the horse. I am aware that until very recently, until this year, in fact, the preponderance of authority has held that the dog *is* cousin to the wolf. But it happens that remarkable and convincing disproof of this old wives' theory has just been adduced by two able and unimpeachable specialists in the field, Charles Quintus Harbison in his *Myths and Legends of the Dog* (Curtis, Webb—$5.00) and D. J. Seiffert in his *The Canidae, a History of Digitigrade Carnivora* (Green & Barton—$3.50). This disposes of this old superstition in a manner that brooks no contradictions. So much for that.

"The history of the dog," Mr. Walker asserts, "is one of greed, double-crossing, and unspeakable lechery." Mr. Walker, who writes with a stub pen, frequently mislays his spectacles, and is inclined to get mixed up now and then, undoubtedly meant to write, "The history of man is one of greed, double-crossing, and unspeakable lechery." If you stopped ten human beings in the street and said to them, "The history of what animal is one of greed, double-crossing, and unspeakable lechery?" seven would say "man," two would walk on hastily without saying anything, and the other would call the police. If you put this same query to ten dogs, none of them would say anything (they are much too fair-minded to go around making a lot of loose charges against men) and none of them would phone the police. (I am reminded to say here, speaking of the police, that no dog has ever held a lantern while a burglar opened a safe belonging to the dog's master. A dog's paw is so formed that he cannot hold a lantern. If your burglar is smart *he* holds the lantern while the dog opens the safe.)

It is true that now and then a dog will double-cross his master. I have been double-crossed by dogs sixteen or eighteen times; eighteen, I believe. But I find in going back over these instances that in every case the fault really lay with me. Take the time that a Scottish terrier of mine named Jeannie let me down; it is a classic but, I believe, typical example. I was living some eight or nine years ago in a house at Sneden's Landing, on the Hudson. Jeannie and her seven pups lived in a pen in the dining room. It would take too long to explain why. The only other person in the house besides me was an Italian cook named Josephine. I used to come out to the house from New York every night by train, arriving just in time for dinner. One evening, worrying about some impending disaster, or dreaming about some old one, I was carried past my station—all the way to Haverstraw, where I had to wait two hours for a train to take me back. I telephoned Josephine from Haverstraw and told her I would not

be able to get there until ten o'clock. She was pretty much put out, but she said she would keep dinner for me. An hour before the train arrived to take me back I got so hungry that I had to eat; I ate several sandwiches and drank two cups of coffee. Naturally when I got home finally and sat down at the dining-room table I had no stomach at all for the wonderful dinner Josephine had kept for me. I ate the soup but I couldn't touch any of the steak. When Josephine set it down before me I said "Wonderful!" in feigned delight and as soon as she went back into the kitchen I cut it up and fed it to Jeannie. We got away with it fine. Josephine was pleased to see my plate licked clean. It looked as if everything was going to be all right and then Josephine set in front of me the largest piece of apple cake I or anybody else had ever seen. I knew how Josephine prided herself on her cake, but I couldn't eat any part of it. So when she went out to the kitchen for the coffee I handed Jeannie the apple cake, hurried to the door which opened from the dining room into the backyard, and put her out, cake and all. Josephine was in high spirits when she saw with what dispatch and evident relish I had disposed of her pastry. It was while I was in the midst of a long and flowery series of compliments on her marvellously light hand with a cake that there came a scratching at the door. Josephine went over and opened it. In trotted Jeannie still carrying the apple cake.

Now it is my contention (although it wasn't at the time) that I double-crossed Jeannie as much as she double-crossed me. After all, I had filled her with steak (she had already had her dinner) and then asked her to consume an enormous slice of apple cake. She was only about a foot, foot and a half, two feet long, and it was too much for her. I should have known this. But, you will ask, why didn't she bury it, for God's sake? And why, I will ask you right back, should she? Dogs are trained to take and carry whatever you hand them that isn't edible, and they are not supposed to go and hide it somewhere. To Scottish terriers apple cake is not edible. Jeannie had no way of knowing how profoundly she was embarrassing me. A French poodle might have sensed the delicacy of the situation that was bound to develop between me and Josephine if an apple cake which I was supposed to have consumed was carried back into the room by a dog, but a Scottie would never have got the idea. Scotties have barely enough brains to get around (in this they are no worse and no better than men, they are just about the same).

As for Mr. Walker's numerous examples of dogs who have broken up affairs, near affairs, and marriages between men and women, I find in a careful examination of each of his instances that it was never the fault of the dog. In every case the dog was simply there and served as an innocent means of revealing the clumsiness of the man and the shallowness of the woman. Let us examine two or three of Mr. Walker's case histories. (1) A man sits down on a lady's dog and kills it. The lady turns on the man and throws him out of her life. Mr. Walker tells the story as if Lucy (I shall call the dog Lucy) had purposely followed the man around trying to trick him into sitting down on her. As a matter of fact the dog was asleep at the time. Now, the obvious point to be made here is that the man was lucky to get rid of that woman. A husband, or a lover, kills about one fifth of the things he sits down on and if he gets a wife, or a mistress, who raises hell about it, he is going to lead a miserable life. This particular dog, at the sacrifice of its life, saved this particular man from an especially nasty fate. I am saddened that Mr. Walker worries about the man in this tragic little triangle. I worry about the dog. The woman, and the man, in this case, might have sighed, after Wordsworth, "Lucy's in her grave and O, the difference to me." But I am reminded of a very acute parody of this famous poem in which the parodist altered only one word, the last. He wrote, "Lucy's in her grave and O, the difference to her." That's the way I look at that.

Case history No. 2: Mr. Walker, calling on a lady whom he intended to take to a masquerade ball, got the lady's dog, a French poodle named Lucille, cockeyed on brandy; in his own words, she was "stiff as a plank." The lady came out of the next room, took the situation in at a glance, and refused to go to the ball. Walker left, without taking the poodle with him. Now I submit that to get a poodle drunk and then walk out on her in the very shank of the evening, leaving her to the harsh mercies of a distraught and indignant mistress, is no way for a gentleman to act. A poodle who has had two brandies (they were forced on her, by the way) is just as eager to go out and make a night of it as you and I are. What is more, on her tenth brandy she will prove to be a hell of a sight better companion than most men and women any of us know. Another thing: as a man who has raised dozens of French poodles (and was fond of all seventy-two of them) I can say on firsthand authority that poodles do not like brandy; all they like is champagne and they prefer it in a metal bowl. The fact that Lucille drank brandy with a guest simply proves what a fine hostess she was while batting for her mistress who was in the next room. Mr. Walker states at the time of this abortive little drinking bout he was dressed as Sir Walter Raleigh. The poodle would have gone with him anyway; poodles are game for anything.

Case history No. 3: "A man I know," writes Mr. Walker, "was visiting a lady when a police dog bit the cook in the calf. The woman thought it was the man's fault for some reason. . . . Nothing came of that romance, either." A lucky thing, too, since the woman was obviously feebleminded, blaming something that happened in the kitchen on a gentleman who was sitting in her parlor. In setting out to draw a dark picture of dogs, Mr. Walker has succeeded in drawing the gloomiest picture of woman known to the literature of our day. The fact that all of them owned dogs is of no more importance or relevance than the fact that they had grandfather's clocks or runs in their stockings. A disturbing little group of ladies, if you ask me.

I do not believe in any such sentimentality as that man's best friend is the dog. Man's best friend is man. A friend is one who cleaves to you in spite of the left side of your nature, the dark and sticky side. The dog never sees that side. To him you are one fine guy, without any faults, and that of course is not true and you can't build a friendship on something that is not true. Among the things that every man treasures about his best friends are their weaknesses, the mistakes they have made, the dilemmas they have got into. These afford any friend a great deal of material with which to regale dinner parties or entertain a group of the fellas at a table in a bar. A dog, not recognizing these weaknesses, mistakes, and dilemmas, never tells anyone about them. A great many of the more famous witty remarks made by New Yorkers in the past ten years were made at the expense of some friend. (Example: Mr. W. remarked of his great friend Mr. R., "He is a dishonest Abraham Lincoln.") A dog has no wit.

One time, going through a kennel in Connecticut where people boarded their dogs, I came across a big, handsome brown water spaniel. He stuck a friendly paw out through the bars of his cage as I walked past, tagged me on the shoulder, and I stopped. I was distressed to discover that he had a huge and ugly swelling on one side of his head. I was surprised that in spite of it he was bright-eyed and gay. Suddenly I found out why. He spit out the swelling. It was a big-league baseball which he had just been holding in one cheek until someone came along to play with him. He got way back in the far end of the cage—only about eight feet it was—and looked at the ball and then at me. I spent fifteen minutes bouncing it at him. He could catch the swiftest bounces and never missed once. He made Rabbit Maranville look like a clumsy, fumbling clown. He reminded me of a bull terrier I once had who could catch a baseball thrown as high in the air as you could throw it. I mean you and you and you. A tough guy named Herb Schorey, who could throw a ball as high as any man I have ever seen, lost five bucks betting Rex couldn't catch a ball *he* threw into the air. These are two dogs I have admired.

Rex I liked better than any dog I have ever known and in another place a few years ago I did him some faint, far justice. But I didn't say then and I don't say now that he was the finest and truest and noblest animal that ever lived. The real dog man likes a dog the way he likes a person; the brightest gleam sometimes comes from the flaw. Rex was a gourmand; he twitched and yelped when he slept; he hated Pomeranians and would chew them to bits although he was five times their size; he killed cats; he jumped on horses when they fell down but never tackled one that was on its feet; if you ordered him to stay home he'd slip out the alley gate and meet you five blocks away; he could lick anything this side of Hell and did; he could chin himself with one paw and lift fifty pounds with his jaws; he had a weakness for chocolate ice-cream cones; and although he learned to open the refrigerator door he never learned to close it. The average good dog is that way: I mean the list of his faults would be longer than the sum of his virtues. All in all, Rex was like the men you are fond of—except that when you kill the men they die. Some-one beat Rex to death one day but he straight-armed the death angel long enough to wobble home. One of his masters wasn't at the house when he got there (Rex was owned by three brothers), so he stayed alive for three hours by some awful, holy effort that I remember after twenty-

Editor's Note: Legendary for his clowning antics, infielder Rabbit Maranville (Walter James Vincent Maranville) was a popular figure in baseball from 1912 until 1935.

five years as clearly as lightning because it was not like anything I have ever seen in the world. When the tardy brother finally arrived home, the dog just managed to touch his hand with his tongue before he dropped dead. Nobody ever more surely earned that long sweet darkness.

If the dog has been ruined for Mr. Walker by fulsome song and silly story, by ornate oration and exaggerated editorial, and by the gibberings of half a dozen ghastly gals, then it has been ruined for him, as I said at the beginning of all this, by men and women and not by dogs.

I have no doubt that the dog can be just as biased and prejudiced as man. I am sure there are some dogs who can't stand men just as there are men who can't stand dogs. I don't see that this proves anything. "I'm always glad," Mr. Fowler said, according to Mr. Walker, "when dogs hate me. It's mutual. When a dog attacks me I know I must be all right."

"When Mr. Fowler attacks *me*," said a prominent dog of my acquaintance recently, "*I* know *I'm* all right. Tell him that when you see him, Mac." I said I would.

DOGS I HAVE SCRATCHED

THERE ARE ONLY A FEW FACTS THAT CAN BE SET DOWN as true of all dogs: they are loyal, they are faithful, they are forgiving. Any other generalization is likely to get you into trouble. If you should say that police dogs are trustworthy guardians of little children, some goldfish-and-parrot lady is likely to come forward with a middle-aged wives' tale about a police dog that turned on a youngster and tore him to pieces. Someone else will then cite instances where youngsters have turned on police dogs and torn them to pieces. If it should be said that dogs lie mournfully on the graves of their masters, somebody will recall a cocker spaniel that was too scared of cemeteries to lie on his master's grave. Ardent spanielists will then loudly contend that the spaniel did not know where his master's grave was. This is silly. He did know where it was. I happen to know he knew where it was. He was too scared to go there. I'm not blaming him; I wouldn't lie on anybody's grave even in the warmest kind of weather. This could hardly be called cowardice.

After all, the line between description and cowardice, intelligence and foolhardiness, instinct and reason is fine, and is drawn by some people here and by others there. A cocker spaniel that attacked an Airedale would be hailed by some as valorous, by others as plain crazy. Cockers are usually fat and short of breath and should go in for gym work and bag punching before taking on the sturdier terriers. But then, that's just my personal opinion. Some would contend that the Airedale would get fat and short of breath before fighting back at a spaniel. I don't know. My point is simply this, however: it is not safe to generalize about dogs. They are as varied as people; lots of them are more varied.

The reason that dogs did not get the upper hand in the misty morning of Time and become the Highest Animal has been explained by Clarence Day in his scholarly treatise *This Simian World*. The dog, loving the slowly evolving supersimian, became his willing slave and lost interest in his own ambitions. I suppose it would be stretching a point to suggest that dogs also had other reasons for not wanting to wrest the power from the apes—that they foresaw, perhaps, how supremacy over the other animals would involve, among other things, riding in the subway, to name but one of the dilemmas that the supermonkey has got himself into. Dogs may have known that as servants instead of masters they would not be allowed in the White House, or in dentists' chairs, or at the last Yale–Harvard game, which was played in a drenching rain that soaked forty or more thousand people to their superior bones. Dogs would, I am confident, have arranged many things better than we do. They would in all probability have averted the Depression, for they can go through lots tougher things than we and still think it's boom time. They demand very little of their heyday; a kind word is more to them than fame, a soup bone than gold; they are perfectly contented with a warm fire and a good book to chew (preferably an autographed first edition lent by a friend); wine and song they can completely forgo; and they can almost completely forgo women.

Of course it is not strictly accurate to say that the supersimian is supreme and that the dog is his slave. It was true once, but not now. A couple of hundred years ago, the first terriers in Scotland were large rangy beasts but they were so amenable to their masters' wishes that they even grew short legs in order to enter the burrows of the animals their masters were fond of hunting down. This abject state of servitude, this willingness to perform miracles for man, has, I believe, long since ceased to motivate dogs. They are by no means turning over in their minds any idea of getting control—for who would wish to inherit the earth now?—but they have evolved various little systems of their own for running this household and that. I know modern dogs, indeed, who exact a definite servitude of their masters, who even call upon them to perform some of the cruder miracles.

One instance will serve. A small black dog named Tessa had a basketful of puppies in a barn. During a cold and wintry night, the puppies, in the midst of a pillow fight or something of the sort, upset the basket and one of them rolled through a wide crack in the barn floor and disappeared. Not having a flashlight or matches, the puppy got farther and farther under the barn. His mother, unable to get him out, for a dog's paws are not capable of using a crowbar as a lever to pry up boards, simply began to scream peremptorily for her master to get up. And in no obsequious or uncertain terms. Her exact words were "Come on out here!" The master, a spare, nervous man, inclined easily to colds, had been in bed for hours—this was around two o'clock in the morning—but he heeded the commands of his dog and came running, in his pyjamas, losing one slipper on the way. With the aid of a shovel, he finally dug the puppy out from under the barn, half frozen. (The master, that is, was half frozen: the puppy had all his clothes on and was quite warm.) There are, of course, stories of dogs who have dug men out of tight places, but I don't see what it would prove if I related them. Besides I personally don't know any. I merely suppose there are some.

It is well to bear in mind that the truth about dogs is as elusive as the truth about man. You cannot put your finger on any quality and safely say, "This is doglike," nor on any other quality and say, "This is not." Dogs are individualists. They react to no set by-laws of behaviorism, they are guided by no strict precepts of conduct, they obey unvaryingly no system of instinct, they follow religiously no standard of bloodlines. I know an English bulldog with the manners of a Chesterfield. I know a beagle that can tell time. I know a Scottie that never has the slightest idea what time it is, and I miserably admit to the ownership of a high-bred French poodle that cools its soup by fanning it with a hat.

W HY NOT DIE?

He has given the lower animals a sixth sense called the "homing instinct." A dog
will travel hundreds of miles to find the master he loves. And so why shouldn't a
man, who is the highest manifestation of God's thought, be drawn intuitively to
his loved ones when they meet again on other planes?
—*From "Why Die?" by Mary Pickford, in Liberty.*

W ELL, THERE ARE SO MANY ANSWERS TO THAT — I MEAN
so many discouraging answers—that I hardly know where to begin. It
might seem presumptuous for me to begin anywhere; and yet I know as
much as the next man about loved ones and I happen to be something
of an authority, in an amateur way, on dogs. I have had dozens of loved
ones and literally hundreds of dogs—a number of which, by the way,
were higher manifestations of God's thought than some of the loved ones
were. I am frank enough to admit that I don't know as much as Miss
Pickford does about other planes, but what I know about dogs may
possibly make up for that.

In the first place, there isn't one dog in a thousand that ever gets
hundreds of miles away from the master he loves, and if he does he ought
to be spoken to sharply when he finally returns home, footsore but happy.
That is, if he finally *does* return home. I have known three Scotties and
a French poodle that couldn't find their way a mile and a half to the

master they loved. One of these Scotties, a worried female, never even discovered that there were two doors to the house she lived in, a front door and a back door. She thought there was only one door. If she sat outside the back door, barking to get in, and you went to the front door, as being handier for you, and whistled and called to her, she wouldn't budge. You had to go out through the kitchen and open the back door for her. She couldn't, in other words, find her way a hundred feet to the master she loved. Of course, it is only fair to add that in the case of this particular Scottie, who was nine years old, there was little love lost between dog and master. This was partly because of the fact that the Scottie, in her later years, had taken to biting an iceman who was bigger than her master, and an uncle who was wealthier.

The homing pigeon, on the other hand, is a dog of another feather. If Miss Pickford had cited the prowess of the homing pigeon as proof of man's immortality and of his certainty to be drawn to loved ones when he has passed away, she would have given me pause. She wouldn't have stopped me completely, but she would have given me pause. The records contain no single instance of a homing pigeon that failed to find its way back to its master or, at any rate, to its cote. There is the classic example of the pigeon whose master wagered five thousand dollars that it could be taken all the way across the United States and released and that it would return unerringly to its home. The gentleman who took the wager—who, in fact, had brought the subject up—had a nefarious little plan by which he hoped to win the money. When hands had been shaken over the bet, this gentleman took the pigeon from its home in New York City to Seattle, Washington, where he clipped its wings and then set it free. Nothing, you see, had been said about not clipping the pigeon's wings. Well, as you may know, the pigeon walked all the way across the country and, six months after it started, walked right up the steps of its master's house in East Sixty-second Street. The mental image of that heroic bird, walking through Seattle, Minneapolis, St. Paul, Milwaukee, Chicago, Cleveland, Buffalo, Syracuse, and, finally, the Bronx and upper Manhattan, is one that I do not want Miss Pickford, and the people who hold with her, to miss. If the thought of a dog travelling a few hundred miles to its master can inspire in such people a belief in the infinite, the thought of that pigeon must inspire in them nothing short of the glorious conviction that all angels will have solid gold wings and make six million dollars a year, tax exempt. Or whatever may be the ultimate ideal of eternal life that they cherish.

It has always been extremely difficult for me to detect anything of human significance, either finite or infinite, in what dogs and birds and other creatures do. To postulate any logical scheme of eternal happiness for man on the instincts of the lower animals is only to become, as you go along, more and more involved and bewildered. For instance, I used to have a dog that could find his way home to me, all right, even over hundreds of miles, but he almost never seemed to know who I was when he got to me. Particularly if I was wearing a cap. He sometimes recognized me when I was wearing a hat, or was bareheaded, but he never recognized me when I was wearing a cap. That would seem to indicate, then—using Miss Pickford's argument—that whereas I may be intuitively drawn to my loved ones when I meet them on other planes, I am not going to like them any more (particularly, I suppose, if they are wearing wings). There I would be, stuck for eternity with a bunch of loved ones for whom I no longer cared.

I am sorry to say that Miss Pickford's brave article did not win me over to a belief in her idea of Heaven or to an acceptance of her basis of reasoning. If I have any beliefs at all about immortality, it is that certain dogs I have known will go to Heaven, and very, very few persons will be there. I am pretty sure that Heaven will be densely populated with bloodhounds, for one thing. It is practically certain that Miss Pickford will not agree with me there. There's no use in us going on with the argument.

To the Editors of *The New Yorker*, SIRS:

When I opened an envelope postmarked Holyoke, Mass., the other day, and addressed to me in the pretty handwriting of a lady named Constance O'Neill, there fell from it a page torn from an article of mine in the issue of your magazine for September 21st. I have learned from long experience that when a page torn from an article of mine drops from an envelope when I open it, the page invariably contains, written on it or clipped to it, proof that some statement or other that I made in the article is not true. In this particular instance there was a paragraph from the Holyoke, Mass., *Transcript* attached to a copy of a piece I had written for *The New Yorker* in which I challenged the ideas and arguments of Miss Mary Pickford about life after death. In that piece, ringed with ink by Miss O'Neill, this statement of mine stood boldly forth: "The records contain no single instance of a homing pigeon that failed to find its way back to its master or, at any rate, to its cote." The newspaper clipping enclosed by Miss O'Neill read, in full, as follows:

HOMING PIGEON REFUSES TO RETURN
TO OWN DOMICILE

Will the owner of homing pigeon No. S264191F kindly call at the home of Mr. and Mrs. Valentine Maternowski, 53 Pine Street, and reclaim the bird?

The pigeon flew in the Maternowskis' kitchen window two weeks ago and lit on a chair. Although released every afternoon since at 3 P.M., the bird has always returned at 6 P.M., after flying around near Holy Cross church. The above number is on a band around one of the pigeon's legs. The Maternowski children have enjoyed feeding the visitor and he has had a whole vacant room to himself.

It certainly looks as if my apologies should be offered both to Miss Pickford and Miss O'Neill, and also to the Maternowskis, who may have been lulled into a false sense of security by my article; who, in fact, may have been living in a fool's paradise as the result of my article. I can just see Mr. Maternowski, as he locked up for the night, after reading my article, saying to Mrs. Maternowski, "Well, dear, it says here that no homing pigeon ever failed to go back home, so I guess we needn't worry about a homing pigeon dropping in on us, anyway." And then one did.

I could have saved my face if I had said "very few instances," but I said "No single instance," which did not leave me the legendary loophole of the exception that proves the rule. I still believe, of course, that I am right about homing pigeons, never having been swayed in an argument in my life, even by facts. It is quite possible that some monkey business, chicanery, or deception has been practiced on me, the Maternowskis, and the pigeon. I know at least three people who would go out of their way to prove me wrong about anything, even if they had to go so far as to trap an ordinary Public Library pigeon, put a numbered band on its leg, and introduce it into the Maternowski home by throwing it through the kitchen window. That may seem a little farfetched and extravagant, but then you don't know the three people I have in mind. Of course, it does seem odd that anyone putting up a game on me about the pigeon would take it all the way to the Maternowksi home in Holyoke, Mass. However, there may be some simple reason for that which evades me for the moment.

There will be an out for me, to be sure, if the pigeon finally returns home, for I didn't say that homing pigeons returned immediately to their masters and their cotes, but the fact that the pigeon has stayed with the Maternowskis for two weeks inclines me to the reluctant belief that it intends to live and die with the Maternowskis. Naturally, I blame the Maternowski children for feeding the pigeon and for giving it a whole vacant room of its own. Very likely the bird enjoyed no such treatment in its own home. It may have had a miserable home life. Who knows but that its master said to it, when he set it free some weeks ago, "Take this message to St. Louis and after that I don't care what you do, only never darken this cote-step again." Homing pigeons are very sensitive and intelligent and understand almost everything you say.

I don't quite get this business about flying around the Holy Cross church for three hours every day. That sounds very much like a mania to me. I suppose there are pigeons in the steeple of the Holy Cross church, but there must have been pigeons in the steeples of lots of other churches that S264191F flew over. The supposition that there is one particular pigeon in the Holy Cross steeple that our homing pigeon fell in love with at first sight is purely sentimental and implies a romantic emotion in homing pigeons which homing pigeons do not have. Homing pigeons always put their work above everything else, or always have until the defection of S264191F.

I do not intend to retract my statement that there is no single instance on record of a homing pigeon failing to return home. Not, at any rate, until I go up to Holyoke and investigate the case myself. I can spot a Library pigeon or a Gertrude Stein pigeon or a church pigeon at a glance. If S264191F does turn out to be an authentic homing pigeon, I shall hand him a small pearl-handled revolver and ask the Maternowskis to leave him alone for a while in that big vacant room.

$\mathcal{M}$Y D A Y
(WITH APOLOGIES TO ELEANOR ROOSEVELT)

OUT OF BED AND AT MY OFFICE AT A QUARTER AFTER
five in the afternoon. Almost everybody was coming down in one elevator
as I was going up in another, since their day had ended and mine had
just begun. Of such contrasts is our country made. I found a man waiting
for me in the reception room. He had been there since three o'clock, and
I was told that he was quite grim and restless, and had said something
to the effect that he would remain in that room until Hell froze over, in
order to confer with me. I am afraid I was more perturbed by the im-
plication of his vehemence than gratified by the realization that whole-
hearted candor and genuine determination are still alive in the land. I
talked with him for five minutes, although how I brought myself to it I
don't know, and I was pleased to discover that he was really waiting for
a man named Turner who works at No. 25 East Forty-fifth Street. My
office is at No. 25 West Forty-third Street. The man had simply made a
mistake.

It has always seemed to me that this East and West business in a
city the size of New York, particularly at this time, when everybody is
beset by doubts and fears of all kinds, should be eliminated. It would be

Editor's Note: From 1935 until 1962, Eleanor Roosevelt wrote her column "My Day," for United Features
Syndicate. It appeared daily, with the exception of its last two years, when it dropped to twice weekly, stopping
seven weeks before her death. Cartoons and parodies often poked fun at this most popular syndication.

nicer if the numbers started at the East River, with No. 1 West Forty-fifth Street, for instance, and continued in that manner over to the North River, the name of which should, of course, be changed to the West River. I know that whenever I walk in a straight line westward from the East River and arrive at the North River, I always have the feeling that I have lost one shoe and have been travelling in a semicircle, the way men do when they are lost in the Arctic. That is called snow blindness. It seems particularly vital that everything in the way of directions and numbers should be made as clear as possible in a day when everybody is concerned about where he is going and who is going to show up.

I sat in my office for an hour or so without turning on the lights. It wasn't as lovely and peaceful as it should have been, considering that twilight had just fallen and all the beautiful golden lights had been turned on in all the offices in the city except mine. My office seemed merely dark and gloomy and a little stuffy, as if someone, perhaps an office boy, had been in there to smoke a cigarette. I must say that I had to smile when I thought that if I had found the boy actually in the room I would have said nothing, particularly if it had been the largest of the boys, a strapping young man named Waldo who always addresses me as "pardner." I believe that this friendliness, regardless of station or title, is the quality that has made this country what it is.

I sat down at my desk and fell to wondering what little animal had given up its life that I might have a cover for my typewriter, and I decided finally that no little animal had, although for the life of me I couldn't think what typewriter covers are made of. I was glad, however, that they do not shoot does, particularly does with young, to make typewriter covers, for it would seem futile and cruel if women deer had to die to make objects which are employed only when the machines they cover are not in use. I thought that if all writers and all other men who use typewriters really worked at it, they would not need covers for their typewriters and the lives of hundreds of thousands of does would be spared.

I had time to read only one of the letters that had come for me, because I had promised to be home for dinner at seven, and I had spent at least an hour and a quarter at the typewriter thinking and writing "Now is the time for all good men to come to the aid of their party." This letter was from the Cleveland Classic (which runs the annual Cleveland Dog Show, in Cleveland, Ohio) and wanted to know if I would be kind enough to send them a night letter "expressing encouragement and general good wishes for the Cleveland Classic Dog Show Luncheon, at the Union Club, Cleveland." It went on to say that the luncheon would be attended by a picked group of Cleveland's one hundred leading industrialists and professional men, and that the "civic event" was to launch a publicity campaign "in behalf of purebred dogs and our dog show." I thought of all the pomp and ceremony that would go on at that luncheon and how simple things are so much simpler, and I wondered who in Cleveland was doing anything about the poor dogs who don't know who their fathers are and whose fathers don't know who they are and don't even remember their mothers. But I suppose that that is the way life goes and all we can do is hope that some day it will no longer go that way or will at least go both ways. The letter was signed "William Z. Breed," and if you do not believe that, you can wire or phone him at No. 16,800 South Park Boulevard, Cleveland, Ohio. He is general manager of the Cleveland Classic.

I went home to dinner and got there at a quarter past seven, which was fifteen minutes later than I had promised, so I showed my wife the letter from the Cleveland Classic and told her I had been delayed pondering it, and although she held it right there in her hand, she did not believe it and wanted to wager that there is nobody named William Z. Breed who is general chairman of the Cleveland Dog Classic. We wrangled about this matter late into the night. Of such unfortunate differences of opinion and unfounded suspicions is married life in this country made up.

THE UPRISING OF THE ANIMALS, AND OTHER OBSERVATIONS OF THE NATURAL WORLD

THE UPRISING OF THE ANIMALS, WHICH I HAVE BEEN expecting for some time, got off to an abortive start in the middle of last November, according to newspaper reports of curious incidents which have just been sent to me by my agents. On November 12th, near Bethlehem, Pa., a six-point buck deer took apart two private residences and a candy store by leaping through plate-glass windows and knocking down, or over, everything he could reach. It seems that he had been minding his own business when the fender of an automobile struck him as he was crossing a road. In one house, after taking care of furniture, vases, and pictures, he went upstairs to finish off the second floor, but was unable to get past a barricade of chairs and tables. He returned to the parlor, smashed a clock and a floor lamp he had overlooked, and made good his escape. No reason, police said, could be assigned for his acts.

Two days later, a so-called pet panther appearing on a radio program

Editor's Note: These four sections first appeared as individual, untitled columns on Thurber's characteristically wide range of subjects. In 1940 and 1941, he wrote and illustrated "If You Ask Me," for *PM*. From 1949 until March of 1952, Thurber sent columns entitled "Letter from the States" to the *Bermudian*.

in Washington, D.C., suddenly leaped at a woman and tore off her mink stole. The lady was uninjured. "I'm out of practice," said the panther. "I misjudged the distance." He was confined in the Washington zoo for life, but he passed the remark, as he was put away, that they would hear from him again. By "they" police believe he meant women. The following day in Texas, a hunter carelessly laid his gun across a chair and was shot in the arm by his dog. Police believe the shooting was an accident, but there seems to be no doubt that the dog put his right front paw in the trigger guard and pulled the trigger. "He moved suddenly," the dog said later to my Texas agent. "I had him full in the sights and he moved."

Police and other authorities who assign reasons for deeds failed to see any significant relationship in this series of events, but it is no secret to my own dog or to me that there was a definite plan on foot in November to overthrow the human species. "Somebody got his dates mixed," my dog explained. "That Texas dog definitely jumped the gun, and the deer and the panther were offside. The uprising was set last spring for November 12, 1950, but there was a serious mistake somewhere down the line." "How many animals are involved in this mutiny?" I asked. "Not mutiny," said my French poodle. "Revolution. You've had your half-century, and we want to take a crack at it in the last half." "Who is in charge of the revolution?" I demanded. "Fala?" "He has his job to do," said the poodle. "Do you think you will succeed in running the world?" I asked. "We can't do worse than you have," the poodle reminded me, and started out of the room. "What was that date again?" I asked. The poodle turned. "November 12, 1950," he said and went out to some meeting or other in the woods.

FLASH. A few hours after I wrote the above, Lowell Thomas described over the air what he called "A Revolution of Dogs" in Milan, Italy. According to his report, a thousand or more canines suddenly attacked the police in the square in front of the Milan cathedral. The story has it that the dogs joined their masters in a violent protest against an increase in the cost of dog licenses. I took the matter up with my French poodle,

Editor's Note: Lowell Thomas, who died in 1981 at the age of eighty-nine, was a popular newscaster and author. He also produced and wrote movie scripts; as early as 1932, he often provided on-camera narration for films.

who had been listening intently to the broadcast with his head cocked to one side. "Well?" I demanded. The poodle sighed. "Off on the wrong paw again," he said, "but it shows what we can do, doesn't it?" "Yes," I said. If you have no pet, and are thinking of buying one, I suggest a canary bird, a stoutly caged canary bird. Look out for rabbits.

Naturalists, who are easily baffled by the behavior of animals, are still wondering today why Big Bill, a polar bear at the Fleishhacker zoo in San Francisco, killed his mate, Min, last Sunday. Bill was lying down, strumming at the headboard with his fingers, dreaming of the ice floes or trying to remember where he had put something, when Min tiptoed into the room. "Tiptoeing again," thought Bill, "like a gahdarn poodle dog." What she said and did in the next few minutes we shall reconstruct later. At the end of it, Bill rolled out of bed and killed her, after which he dragged her thirty feet to a pool of water and held her under for several minutes, to make sure.

I saw the male polar bear at the Central Park zoo duck his mate one Sunday last April. He grabbed her ear, pulled her head under, kept her there ten seconds or so, and then let her go, growling, half playfully, "That's for nothing." The Central Park polar bears seem to like each other, which is a break for the zoo attendants, the homicide squad, and the female bear.

Perhaps the principal trouble with American zoos, as regards bears, is that the men in charge of them think that all female bears look alike to a male bear. This conclusion, arrived at from the premise that all female bears look alike to the men in the zoo, is unfortunate to the point of being deadly. To a male polar bear, female polar bears are as different as thumbprints to a G-man. A male polar bear likes only about one female in every fifty he comes across in a day's courting swim. Some bears swim seventy-five miles along a bear-infested coast before they find a female cute enough to bother with. Not knowing this, the Fleishhacker zoo-men brought Bill a mate last spring that he couldn't abide. She put starch into everything she washed and cheese into everything she cooked; what is more, she kept scratching constantly. Bill swatted her out of existence one day as nonchalantly as if she had been a fly.

He was still grumbling about mating conditions in California when the Fleishhacker people brought him still another mate, rousing him from dreams of the Arctic, where a man can have his pick of a thousand gals. "Lookit, Bill," they said, cheerfully, "the lady of our choice!" Bill noted that she smelled faintly like a Los Angeles roadateria, and that she tacked slightly to the left in lumbering, which was going to be bad since he tacked to the right. Furthermore, she giggled. When the zoo-men left, Bill told the newcomer to stay out of his way, and he went back into the cave and lay down.

When Bill did not come out for several days, Min took to tiptoeing in to see if he wanted a glass of water. She would fiddle with doilies, empty ashtrays, wash out his briar pipe with soap and water, open the window if it was shut and shut it if it was open. Once she felt his forehead to see if he had a fever and Bill took a cut at her, but missed. She fled, screaming.

When Bill didn't come out for several more days (he felt fine, but he didn't want to come out), she decided that he was sick and she determined to take his temperature. She tiptoed in and stuck a thermometer in his mouth before he knew what was happening. Bill watched her tidy up his bureau, putting his socks, handkerchiefs, and shirts, which had all been in one drawer, neatly into separate drawers. When she started hanging his ties on a patented nickel-plated cedarwood tie rack which clasped them in such a way that you couldn't get them off unless you knew how to work the automatic clip-shift tie-release, Bill leaped out of bed and roared into action. He finished off her, the thermometer, and the tie rack before anybody could stop him. "They turned hoses on me," he said later, "and that helped. I was getting pretty hot."

The Fleishhacker people are probably out looking for another mate for Big Bill right now. Well, I have done all *I* can.

"*People* have more fun than anybody," says Colonel Stoopnagle on the radio all the time. Forty-six years of quiet—or fairly quiet—research by me have proved that this is not so. Among the creatures which have more fun than people are the wood duck, the plover, the beagle, the kangaroo (with or without boxing gloves), the snail, the egret, and the red squirrel.

There was a family of red squirrels in the walls of a country house I lived in this winter. From the sounds I used to listen to as I lay awake at night in the dark, I figured that these squirrels, after a jolly day spent in leaping from tree to tree and eating birds, played more than fifty different kinds of games after sundown, including soccer, roulette, checkers, throw-the-shoehorn, jump-in-the-pan, hide-in-the-dark, skittles, roll-the-bottle, pussy-wants-a-corner, handball, football, and you-chase-me.

And here's another thing. The red squirrel, like all other animals except the human being, is not only fully dressed when he wakes up in the morning but fully dressed when he goes to bed at night. There is no more fun in the world than this.

No animals except the human being try to destroy their own species,

Editor's Note: Colonel Lemuel Q. Stoopnagle (whose real name was F. Chase Taylor) was one of radio's earliest satirists. He appeared as part of the "Stoopnagle and Budd" comedy team, which began broadcasting in 1931 and aired for over a decade.

and this in itself proves that anybody has more fun than people. Not long ago, in Canada, along a thirty-six mile front, thousands of ducks known as buffleheads, who were migrating at night, crashed to the earth. Many of them were killed and most of the survivors were injured. Nobody seems to know how so many buffleheads could all get off the beam at once. It is claimed that the bufflehead is not terribly well equipped for flying on account of the fact that God, in a moment of whimsy, placed the duck's legs too far back to assure him a good balance. As a result, the bufflehead cannot take off from where he is sitting, like the cedar waxwing or the evening grosbeak, but has to skitter over a long stretch of water before he can rise, like a transatlantic Clipper. The point I am trying to work up to here is that while the buffleheads may crash to earth by the thousands, they are not filled with bullets which they have poured into each other. In this way they differ from people, who have so much fun.

Buffleheads, by the way, are also known as butterballs. I didn't tell you this before because I was afraid you wouldn't believe it. I didn't want you to get the idea that I just sit here making up stories about buffleheaded butterballs whose legs are built too far back. This discovery may have been made by scientists whose stomachs are built too far forward, but it is apparently true. The story appeared in the New York *Herald Tribune*, which, of course, believes that everything is crashing to the ground in the dark, but which seems to have got the tragic tale of the buffleheads from a sober and authentic, if somewhat astonished, source.

The only animals I have ever seen attack each other en masse for no good reason, like the human being, were a group of guinea pigs owned by the Board of Health of the city of Columbus, Ohio. I used to visit the laboratories every day, as a reporter, and one morning the Negro attendant there said to me, "I can make all those twenty guinea pigs fight by striking two empty milk bottles together." Before wagering any money on the probable falsity of this remarkable statement, I telephoned a man named John McNulty, a connoisseur of the improbable, futile, and uncalled-for aspects of the behavior of animals.

"Have these pigs," asked Mr. McNulty, "been consorting with human beings for any considerable period of time, such as forty-eight hours, maybe?" I told him they had known the company of people for several months. "Five will get anybody ten," said McNulty, "that there isn't anything these pigs won't do, no matter what you strike together." A few moments later, the Negro attendant struck two empty milk bottles together and twenty guinea pigs jumped at each other, screaming and cursing, scratching and biting and pulling knives.

The point here, in case you have been striking matches and looking for it, is that those guinea pigs had had more fun than people until they got mixed up with people. Then they became irritable, petulant, threatening, pugnacious, and bent on the destruction of their own species.

I am sure that all of my listeners, including the younger children, can think of eleven hundred reasons why anybody has more fun than people. Send them in, accompanied by a human scalp, and this station will send you a black cocker spaniel with a red ribbon in his hair, providing you do not let him associate with people. People raise more hell than anybody.

By listening at keyholes from time to time, when I have something better to do, I have heard two rumors or reports about myself: (1) I was a mediocre newspaper reporter, afraid to get my foot in the door, too restless to listen to anybody, and unable to estimate property losses in a fire within two hundred thousand dollars of the actual amount; (2) I know nothing about a farm, although I own one, and I can't tell a chicken hawk from a china auction. Both charges are untrue, but let's take on the crack about the farm first, and get around to the other some other time.

Just because I am a man of the world, at ease in the company of the international set—I can carry on a conversation in French entirely in the present tense and deal with both reminiscence and prophecy—certain churls have got the idea that I am not at home with nature and the soil. It happens that my mother's ancestors were mainly farmers, and that her paternal grandfather once owned fifty thousand acres of land. This is admittedly 49,945 more than I own, but his Ohio was larger than my Connecticut. Anyone who owned fifty thousand acres in Connecticut would have a piece of both Bridgeport and Hartford.

When I was ten I could hitch a horse, load a rifle, and take a cream separator apart. If I did not drive the first, shoot the second, or put the third back together again, it is because I knew the value of caution, a trait rarely found in the average impetuous farm boy. I could tell the difference between a brown thrasher and a McCormick reaper, and I could call hogs, one of whom usually glanced over his shoulder to see what it was. Now that I am fifty, I leave the outdoor work on my Cornwall farm to two younger men, to whom I occasionally give advice. I have, naturally, a stock of useful facts, helpful hints, and shrewd guesses about the phenomena of country life. Let us look at a few of these.

1. If the porch wren, whose song goes "churtle-urtle-urtle, eet-eet-eet" is not back by May 1st, he is either dead or he found a nicer place near Stamford.

2. Never approach anything in the dark that is breathing heavily.

3. If you try to count the number of whips a whippoorwill can make without stopping to inhale, you will never drop off to sleep.

4. Do not kill robins with a flyswatter to keep them from eating the strawberries. It isn't manly.

5. Everything that sounds the way you think a corncrake should sound is not a corncrake.

6. Do not fire through the front door every time somebody knocks after midnight. It might be old Mrs. Detweiler.

7. If you can hear it moving but you can't see it, leave it alone.

8. If you can't see it or hear it any longer but your dog can, it's still there.

9. If a deer gets into the garden and eats your best greens, ask him to go away. This works as well as anything else I've tried.

10. This final hint is borrowed from the *Herald Tribune*: "A lady whose lettuce and radish beds were being raided by rabbits planted a border of empty pop bottles with the necks about three inches above ground. Even in a slow wind, she reports, the mournful whistling is enough to scare the small thieves away."

This lady's ingenious scarebunny would merely amuse Bancroft, an old experienced woods rabbit with one broken ear, who has been sharing my lettuce crop with me for many years on a fifty-fifty basis. The rabbits are tough up here in Connecticut. Spike Jones' band might conceivably annoy Bancroft, but it wouldn't frighten him. He isn't even afraid of me.

I just realized that I have not explained Fig. 1, and you may possibly be wondering what it is. Fig. 1 is a cow, drawn freehand from memory. It doesn't actually illustrate anything in this letter. It is merely an ornament, named Mildred.

Fig. 1.

The (Cold) War between the Sexes

"Could you play something just a tiny bit hotter this time, Mr. Ranoldi?"

(BATTLE STATIONS)

"I suppose that subconsciously he didn't really want to come."

"You go back to the party, Mr. McMurtrie, I'll handle him.*"*

"He's unmasking her ideology."

"*Don't you remember? I was here three nights ago with a lady who beat me up.*"

"*I could go on like this forever!*"

"Why don't you young people play Post Office?"

"Are you listening to me, or aren't you?"

"Don't you feel drawn to me, Mr. Burke, at all?"

"The magic has gone out of my marriage.
Has the magic gone out of your marriage?"

"*She'll spoon with any man that comes along.*"

"I'd give the world to be sultry, but I just succeed in looking sleepy."

"She's bankrupt in every way except financially."

"*I've gone nudist, Mr. Ballinger. Do you mind?*"

*"Nothing you wore could ever change
my feeling for you, Miss Sargent."*

*"Those dry points I was speaking of are
in this next room, Mr. Norris."*

"Sweets?"

"She's sex-starved."

"If I told you a dream I had about you, Mr. Price, would you promise not to do anything about it unless you really want to?"

"Won't you put your burdens on me?"

Marriages are made in Heaven.

Divorces are okay in Hell.

"*Mine!*"

"Sunday, April fifth, was the last the children and I ever saw of him."

"*I love him, Father, and he loves me, and we came here to tell you!*"

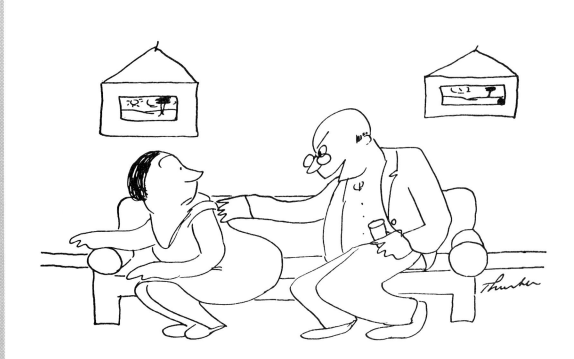

"You destroy the scientist in me, Miss Blair, and bring out the man."

"I could find the chink in your armor if I were given time."

"It's wonderful to get away from women in every shape and form."

"Now don't you worry for a minute—I'll drive the car."

"*How large is your family, Madam?*"

"I have an awful foreboding that eventually I'll succumb to you
but I feel I owe it to my conscience to put up an awful fight."

I

IT'S LIGHTER THAN YOU THINK

A LETTER FROM ROGER

LAST MONDAY I SHOULD SIMPLY HAVE HAD MY NOON-time sherry and bitters and gone back to bed, had it not been for Mr. Roger Scott, manager of the Dawn Auto Club, of Chicago. He had thoughtfully mailed me, on Saturday, a lovely fat letter, with eight enclosures, and it arrived in the early mail Monday. The first things that dropped out when I opened it were a check for thirty-seven hundred dollars and a telegram notifying me that I was the winner of a Buick sedan and cash. "Congratulations!" said the telegram. "You won Grand First Prize and $1,000 for promptness." Of course I began to suspect right then that there must be some mistake, for whereas everybody admits that I am the soul of honor, it is common knowledge that I am too wistful to be prompt. The telegram went on to say, however, that Mr. Scott would pay all round-trip expenses for myself and a Companion to come to Chicago and get my prize. I was to wire the time of my arrival. If I didn't care to come to Chicago, I could have the check for thirty-seven hundred dollars sent to me. Since I already had the check, I began to get a little confused, and so I examined the enclosures more carefully. It turned out that the check was just a sample check and telegram a sample telegram. I was urged not to feel badly about this but to feel happy. A careful reading of the other six enclosures, I was assured, would show me that although the check was no good, I should soon get one that would be good.

I don't expect to make the whole proposition entirely clear to you, because it never became entirely clear to me, although I spent several hours going over the various enclosures. It was unquestionably unfortunate that, of those which remained, I began on one entitled "Magic Sales Card for Helen Dawn Toiletries." I can see now that this was not an enclosure for beginners but an enclosure for advanced students. It threw me off terribly. In the first place, on the back of the Magic Sales Card were pictures of six bubbles, each about the size of a half-dollar. They were labelled as follows: "Pull Ruth Receipt," "Pull Irene Receipt," "Pull Jane Receipt," "Pull Laura Receipt," "Pull Evelyn Receipt," and "Pull Julia Receipt." Each bubble was perforated so that it could be pulled loose from the Magic Card. A notice in red said: "Choose your favorite name." My favorite name—Rosemary—didn't happen to be there, which was just as well because, on reading the directions further, I discovered that somebody else was supposed to pull the receipts. "On the back of each Bubble," these directions read, "is printed the name and special price of a toilet preparation. Just pull off a Bubble receipt. Pay the special price printed on the back to the person having this card. When the toiletries arrive the agent will deliver your selection."

By this time I was thoroughly alarmed. There seemed to be no doubt that the agent referred to was myself and that I would have to go around delivering toiletries to people. In a kind of minor panic, I went on to another enclosure, a Guarantee Prize Bond, very impressively got up, like a cross between a court summons and a thousand dollars in stage money. In one corner was a place for me to sign my name. Here my natural caution stood me in good stead, for I didn't sign. It turned out that if I had signed I would have laid myself open to receiving for free examination the Good Luck Assortment as follows: 1 tube Dawn's toothpaste, 1 tube Helen Dawn cold cream, 1 tube Dawn's shaving cream, 1 Sifter Can Deodorant powder, 1 bottle Helen Dawn perfume, and 1 large box Helen Dawn face powder. When these arrived I was to send two dollars within ten days, whereupon I was to be credited with 99 more Points in the Dawn Auto Club, thus making my total 999 Points toward winning a Buick, $1,500 in gold, and $1,000 for promptness. You can imagine my excitement when I discovered that, with 999 Points, all I would need to win the Grand First Prize was one more Point!

After going over the Guarantee Bond a second time, however, I was still anything but clear about the Point system. For one thing, I couldn't figure out how I happened to have 900 Points already, without turning a hand, so I went on to the next enclosure.

This was a large colored circular which, when unfurled, measured two feet by a yard in size, and contained a map of the United States, pictures of a bride in her wedding gown, a group of students in mortarboards, a bungalow in the country, a ship at sea, and photographs of Louis Snowbank of Minneapolis and twenty-four other persons, including a nine-year-old boy. This circular not only failed to clarify the Point system at all, but simply threw the whole thing into the wildest sort of confusion. I folded it up and picked up still another enclosure, which began: "During the past season I called at your residence in Connecticut and talked with you about your shade and fruit-tree situation. There are several feature Maple and Elm trees about your residence which are very valuable to the setting." Luckily, before I got all tangled up in that, I discovered that it was a separate letter, which I had opened at the same time as Roger Scott's letter and had inadvertently placed among the Scott enclosures.

The next genuine enclosure was, it came out, the one I should have read first. It was the letter proper from my friend Roger Scott and began "Dear Friend." (He can never think of my first name, but then I am just as bad about faces.) The Proposition now began to shape up a little, for Scott came right out and said that he wanted me to advertise his products in my neighborhood. Roger told me that I had been selected for the opportunity to win a Buick 8 Sedan. "You have already been awarded an official score of 900 Points," he wrote, which cleared up the 900 Points. "The enclosed Grand Prize Certificate proves and guarantees your standing for the Buick and Cash—or you may have $3,700 if you prefer all cash instead of the Sedan." The letter then went on to outline the Friendship Advertising Plan. "In a recent Friendship Advertising Campaign," Roger wrote, "we paid $2,100 to Fred Gardner, Osceola, Iowa."

At first I thought that it must have been through Gardner that Roger and I had met, for I know a Fred Gardiner in Columbus, Ohio, but I don't suppose it is the same person, although it might be.

Toward the end of his chummy letter, Roger quoted the telegram again, in full—the one congratulating me on winning the Grand First Prize. Once more I was fooled into thinking that I had really won, but Roger explained that these Glorious Words, this Welcome Message, will be flashed over the wires to someone, and that it may be myself. Once more I felt pretty low and was just going to call for my sherry and bitters when I ran across this sentence in his letter: "I'm going to have your nearest Buick dealer select the latest model Sedan, fill it with oil and gas, and turn it over to you and hand you the keys." Apparently, after all, my 900 Points had won the Buick, whether I got the $1,500 Cash and the $1,000 promptness bonus or not. To say that I was frightened is putting it mildly. Nothing in the world would terrify me so much as having a Buick delivered at my office. I simply cannot and will not drive in traffic. It's all I can do to drive in the country. And here Roger wanted to deliver to me, in West Forty-fifth Street, right in the heart of town, a big sedan. I couldn't just leave it standing there. If I started to drive it off, as I probably would when a cop bawled at me to get ahn outa there, I'd very likely crash at Sixth Avenue and kill somebody.

Fortunately, there proved to be a way out. "If you can't take advantage of this offer," Roger said in a postscript. "Please hand all papers to someone who would like to win $3,700." This is exactly—or almost exactly—what I did. I handed to a man at Fifth Avenue and Thirty-second Street all papers except the check for thirty-seven hundred dollars. I still think that maybe I won.

I BREAK EVERYTHING I TOUCH

I AM INTERESTED IN FORMING A LITTLE CLUB OF miserable men. No man can belong to it who can fix anything or make anything go. No man can belong to it who is handy around the house— or the garage, or anywhere else.

I was born with an aversion to tools. When I was in the eighth grade I had to go to manual-training class every Thursday and I was still planing away at a breadboard when the other boys were putting the finishing touches on kitchen cabinets, davenports, and pianos. The breadboard was as far as I ever got and when I finally had it done the instructor, a temperamental and highly strung man named Buckley, who really loved carpentry and cabinetmaking, picked it up and looked at it and said, "Thurber, I weep for you." I wept for me, too. I was covered with cuts and bruises from gouges, planes, bits-and-braces, saws, and hatchets. None of the other boys had a mark on them.

The only thing I can really do is change the ribbon on a typewriter, but it took me twenty-two years to learn that and every now and then I have to call in a friend or neighbor to help unravel me. When I was younger, I once changed a fuse in the fuse box, but I am too old and too smart to try that again. They tell me that electricity has been harnessed, and I say yes and so was King Kong. I don't even like to monkey with the thermostat that regulates the oil furnace. Every time I put the thing down to 55° before going up to bed, I expect to be blown out through the roof.

I come by my ineptitude with contraptions of any kind quite naturally. My grandmother on my mother's side was afraid of doorbells; she always took the receiver off the telephone hook during a thunderstorm; she believed that if you unscrewed an electric light bulb, electricity would drip invisibly all over the house and if you then struck a match, you would be blown to Hell. My mother was confident that the Victrola we bought in 1913 would explode if you wound it too tight, and she was forever warning me not to drive the family Reo without gasoline, because she had heard it was bad for it if you did.

About the only thing I really know about an automobile is that you can't run it without gasoline. The Lord knows that enough of my men friends have explained the principles of the gas engine to me, but I am always just where I was when they started—and so is the gas engine. For all I know, the distributor regulates the pressure on the manifold. I can run a car and I can stop one; I can also turn right and left and back up; but I don't know exactly what is happening. The thing has never become any more clear to me than the third law of thermodynamics—or the first one, as far as that goes.

I have, of course, been in any number of embarrassing situations with automobiles, from my grandfather's old Lozier to my 1935 Ford. In England (I drove fifteen thousand miles in Europe and lived to tell it) my battery went dead near one of the cathedral towns, and I phoned a garage. A young mechanic in a truck appeared after a while and said he would pull me and I could get my engine started that way. I had been pulled and pushed in the old Reo days and I knew that you could start the engine that way. I knew that you pushed the clutch in (or is it out?) and then let it out (or in) suddenly. So the garage man attached a rope to the back of his truck and to the front of my car and away we went— over the hills and through the dales of England.

Every quarter mile or so he would stop and come back to me to see what was the matter. He lifted the hood, he got under the car, but there was nothing doing.

At the end of five or six miles he got out and said, "What gear you got her in?" He had me there. I didn't have her in any gear. I had her in neutral. He just stared at me, not in anger or resentment, not with an injured look, but as Cortez must have stared when he stumbled on the Pacific. I know now that you can't make her turn over if you've got her in neutral, but I don't know why. You can make her turn over with the starter when you've got her in neutral. The hell with it.

My worst embarrassment came one day in Connecticut when my engine began to heat up until the red fluid in the gauge was almost up to the top. I stopped at a garage and pointed this out to a mechanic. I got out of the car and stood looking in at the dashboard, thus seeing it from an unfamiliar angle.

Suddenly I saw what I thought was the matter. A needle on one of the dials pointed to 152. "For God's sake!" I said to the mechanic, "that shouldn't be registering so high, should it?" (I always swear around mechanics to make them think I have an easy, profane knowledge of motors.) The garageman gave me a long, puzzled look—the old Cortez look. "That's your radio dial, brother," he said.

Sure it was. I just hadn't recognized it. Half the time I look at the oil-pressure gauge instead of the speedometer and I think I am doing only seventeen miles an hour.

One of the presents I got for Christmas was a handsome newfangled soda syphon complete with a set of directions. I put the thing away until just the other day, and then I got the directions out and looked at them, the way ladies look at the snakes in a zoo.

The first three directions were simple enough but the fourth began to make me suspicious. It reads like this: "Place a Super-Charger in the charge holder with small end pointing out (see Figure C). Then screw back cap of charge holder. Do not use force." They don't know that the first thing I use is force—I use it on linked-nail puzzles and olive bottles and everything else. An engineer or a mechanic or my brother-in-law or the next-door neighbor would go about a thing like this simply and gently, but what I do is get panic-stricken, the way you would if somebody grabbed you in a dark room, and the first thing you know I have the contraption on the floor with my knee on its chest. Pretty soon something makes a sharp snapping noise and the device has to be taken to the attic to join all the other contrivances whose bones I have broken in a series of unequal struggles. Psychologists would explain this by saying that I don't really want the things around so I break them while pretending to be trying to make them work. Psychologists are often right.

But to get back to the syphon. Rule Six says: "To puncture Super-Charger and to charge the syphon push down charging button (marked A in Figure D) with heel of hand (see Figure E); or give button a tap with palm of hand. Some people find it easier to push charging button against edge of kitchen sink or table." I haven't got up enough courage yet to experiment with this syphon, for while I am sure it would work fine for nine men out of ten, I have a feeling it would fight to a draw with me. Next year the makers might even have to add a line or two to Rule Six: "Mr. Thurber of Woodbury, Connecticut, finds it easier to grasp the syphon with both hands and whang it against the kitchen stove. See Group F: the cut and bleeding figure is Thurber."

When I was twelve years old, an uncle gave me a little box Brownie, the simplest camera in the world. A folder of directions came with it, and I warily approached the section where it explained how to put in a film. "First," it said, "spring out the spool pins." I knew right there the thing had me. I knew that far from being able to spring out the spool pins, I wouldn't be able to find them. I gave the camera to the first little boy I met on the street, a youngster of eight, who I was sure could spring out the spool pins with his eyes blindfolded and mittens on his hands.

This is not the world for me, this highly mechanized world. I can only hope that in Heaven there is nothing more complicated than a harp and that they will have winged mechanics to fix mine when I get down and break its back.

"*Will you brace up or will I come over there?*"

"He broke a chain letter and he's scared of every sound."

"*He comes in here and sits all alone.*"

"*Well, you can't wait for the upturn in* here."

"*Let's dance this!*"

*"Don't keep saying 'God forbid' every time
I mention Mr. Roosevelt!"*

"All right, all right, all right. You're for Roosevelt. I don't go around trying to win you over to Dewey all the time, do I?"

"I wish she'd go to town, don't you?"

"*I'd like to get my hands on the astrologer who told you that!*"

"We're trying to get drunk, but our heart isn't in it."

"And I say velouté sauce is nothing but white chicken gravy!"

"She's out of fix because they've cleaned up the movies."

"*Are there any—cucarachas?*"

"*George! I think I got it straightened out now!*"

"Come on, get hot!"

 MORE ICE ADDED TO U.S. AS THOUSANDS CHEER

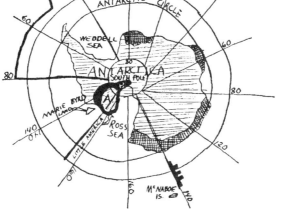

To a great many people, including myself, the newspaper accounts of Admiral Byrd's latest discoveries in the Antarctic a week or so ago made little, if any, sense. I confined my own study of the involved explorations to the *Herald Tribune* article. I reread this article many times and pored over the map that went with it, but for two or three days, I couldn't make out what had actually been done and how it had been accomplished. All that I knew for sure was that Byrd had reported to President Roosevelt (who hasn't enough to worry him the way it is) that the recent discoveries had added approximately two hundred thousand square miles of ice to American ice possessions at the South Pole.

I was determined to keep on trying to figure out the article and the map. First I made a map of my own, copying it from the *Herald Tribune* map but making it simpler. My map, for instance, has only thirteen radiating lines, or parallels, as against the *Herald Tribune*'s eighteen. This makes the thing a little less confusing, without detracting from the clarity of the chart, because the five lines I left out are of no importance. Nor, indeed, are the thirteen I left in. I would have erased them after I had my map done, but India ink will not erase. I am afraid these parallels are going to handicap my story of the explorations, because they are likely to give the reader the effect of looking at the map through the top of a birdcage.

We now know approximately where we are, without being too technical, but there are one or two other matters regarding the map which I must explain before we get back to Admiral Byrd, if I can find him. The little island at the bottom marked McNaboe Island was marked Macquarie Island on the *Herald Tribune* map and probably is Macquarie Island, but I print my letters so large I couldn't get Macquarie in without running the last two letters into the battleship (lower right). This battleship was not on the newspaper map, and I put it in merely because I had made the mistake of drawing my map from the bottom upward instead of the top down, a system which is bound to cause the heel of the drawing hand to come into contact with, and smudge, lines which have been drawn but have not yet dried. To cover up the smudge I made, I turned it into a battleship. Let it serve as a warning to the Japanese that we do not intend to give up the four hundred thousand square miles of ice we own down there without a struggle.

Now to get back to what actually happened on Byrd's last flight of exploration and discovery. The black area marked B on the map indicates the new ice that has been added to American possessions by the Admiral's recent activities. The dotted area marked A represents the ice that Byrd had discovered previously. It will be noticed at once that the newly discovered ice completely surrounds the previously discovered ice, and a moment's thought will lead one to wonder how this could be. I couldn't figure it out myself for a long time, but finally I decided that that's what comes from exploring in airplanes. You can fly right over something without discovering it, discover something farther on, and then come back and discover what, if you had been on dog sledges, you would have been bound to discover first.

But we *must* get back to what Byrd actually did. He found out, for one thing (and I am going strictly by the newspaper account) that Marie

Byrd Land (A and B) is "a high area with an elevated ice plateau." I had supposed that everybody knew that already, but it seems no. The region, continues Byrd's wireless, is "wholly glaciated and overridden by an ice sheet, presumably to a great depth." This also seems to have come as a surprise to Byrd and his men, but I fancy that President Roosevelt, who is very quick mentally, had suspected it all along. The principal result of Byrd's explorations, however (and I'm *still* sticking to his report to the papers), was the discovery that a long-sought transcontinental strait which was supposed to lie beneath the ice probably does not lie beneath the ice at all, although *maybe* it does. The strait is there, or something like a strait is there (Byrd calls it a passage or depression), but it is, the Admiral says, "more apparent than real." That is, it has reality but is also imaginary. In other words, it is something like spots before the eyes, only more icy and expansive. Just because one cannot reach out and touch the spots before one's eyes, it does not prove the spots are not there; and, conversely, simply because one sees them, it does not prove they *are* there.

Byrd established, he says in his report, that "not far east of this strait (or passage) and to the north and south the plateau descending from Marie Byrd Land curved around and to the south, so that no such passage could exist." I have been over that sentence a dozen times, and I have finally come to the conclusion that Admiral Byrd was lost. I think he was lost, and I think he was too proud to say so. After all, he had been gone on this flight six hours and forty-four minutes and he had to say *something* when he got back.

Another thing the Admiral discovered (and this seems to be the most important discovery of all) is that "from the 75th parallel [never mind seeing the map] to the Pole, a stretch of 1,000 miles, it is all land, overwhelmed by ice to be sure, but land anyhow." Of course, this overwhelm of ice is several thousand feet thick and always will be, but President Roosevelt will be glad to know that underneath it all there is land. To be sure, we cannot get at the land, but it belongs to us and always will belong to us, unless, of course, there should some day come a huge ice slide which would cause all the ice to move away from the South Pole, like a tremendous glacier, leaving the land bare. In that case it is doubtful whether the United States could establish its claim to the land, because, after all, Byrd stuck the American flag in the ice. In some cases he didn't come within a mile of the land underneath. I should think, therefore, that in the event the ice did move off, Byrd or somebody else (and I have an idea it would be Byrd) might have to go back and reclaim all the land for America by sticking flags in it. Furthermore, if the ice we now own should, in moving off, end up on the shores of Australia, say, and finally completely cover that continent, I doubt very much that Great Britain would even recognize our claim to the ice, let alone our claim to the land underneath it (Australia).

To return to the map for a moment (and if anybody has been wondering, I haven't the slightest idea what the heavy black zigzag line means), you will notice that compared to the great expanse of shaded area marked Antarctica, Byrd's ice accumulations so far are absolutely trivial. Everything shown on this map is ice, or ice-and-land, or ice-on-land, except the white areas, which are water (note Ross Sea and Weddell Sea—named for the mysterious and inaccessible old Weddell house). My estimate may be wrong, because there was no scale of miles on the map I copied, but I should judge that if the whole shaded area (Antarctica, or Marie Byrd Land) is finally discovered and claimed for America, we will possess, in all, about 28,700,000 square miles of ice. It is not a thing to contemplate blandly. It is high time that America woke up and realized that every year hundreds of thousands of square miles of ice are being added to her possessions, and that our pride in this accumulation is, after all, based on no sounder reason than that somewhere underneath all this ice there lies, or may lie, some land. Are we landowners or ice dealers? Are we men or penguins? Let us face these questions soberly.

"You must understand," said Rear Admiral Byrd, "that it will take months and months to tabulate the findings we made in Antarctica. The data will appear in four volumes, when completed."

"Surely," said Senator Grosbeak, "surely. What this committee had in mind was simply an outline."

"You see," said Senator Vanfield, "you have claimed one hundred and twenty-five thousand square miles of land for the United States, and we'd like to be able to give people some idea of what we've got down there, when they ask us. They've been asking us ever since you got back."

"Exactly," put in Senator Golldring. "What's *on* all this land down there, anyway? The newspapers have been pretty sketchy."

"Ice is on it," said Byrd. "In some regions there is no land, just ice. We claimed one area of floating sheet ice which is as large as France."

"That seems like a lot of sheet ice," said Senator Grosbeak. "We don't need that much sheet ice, do we?"

"It comes with the rest of the land," Senator Eakin told him.

"Well, now, how about minerals?" asked Senator Vanfield. "What did you find in the way of minerals?"

"In the way of minerals—and they consist largely of hypothetical coal," said the Rear Admiral, "stand impenetrable ice caps of from twelve hundred to two thousand feet in depth."

"That's going to be bad," said Senator Golldring.

"Anthracite you say this coal is, eh?" asked Senator Grosbeak, who was slightly deaf.

"He said it was *hypothetical*," Senator Eakin said, in Grosbeak's ear.

"How about oil, copper, and the like?" asked Senator Golldring.

"The geological findings were most valuable," said Byrd. The senators all sat up. "In addition to coal-bearing rocks of the Permo-Carboniferous Age, there is a very rich Jurassic fossil, Tertiary fossils, Cretaceous ammonites, leucite-basalt, and a few slopes strewn with quartzite, mica-schist, and gneiss. All of extreme value to the student."

"To the student, eh?" said Senator Grosbeak. There was a deep silence.

"*What can we do* with this gneiss?" asked Senator Vanfield.

"They make lenses out of it," said Senator Grosbeak. Senator Eakin urged his chair a little closer to Grosbeak's. "You're thinking of 'Zeiss,' " he said.

"Gneiss," began Rear Admiral Byrd, "may be either igneous or metamorphic; it contains quartz and feldspar—orthoclase, microcline, and plagioclase—as well as chlorite, muscovite, biotite, and so on."

"But no oil, eh?" asked Senator Golldring. "We need oil."

"If there were oil in Antarctica, it would be impossible to get at it unless the region became tropical or semitropical again, as it once was."

"How long would that take?" asked Senator Grosbeak.

"Several hundred million years," said Byrd. There was a long silence and all the senators looked slightly unhappy.

"It might take only *one* hundred million years," said the Rear Admiral, reassuringly.

"How about birds—are there any valuable birds down there?" asked Senator Vanfield.

"The only bird life is penguins," said Byrd.

"Since *you* came back—hah, Admiral?" laughed Senator Grosbeak—and he shoved his elbow into Senator Eakin's side. Senator Eakin moved his chair slightly away.

"Fortunately for the preservation of these harmless and delightful birds," went on the Admiral, "their blubber-coated skins do not possess a marketable value."

"What'd he say?" asked Senator Grosbeak, who was still chuckling at his bon mot.

"Blubber-coated penguins," said Eakin, "valueless."

"There are also millions of seals," continued Byrd, "but they are not fur-bearing and are also happily immune from human exploitation. There are millions of seals."

"I don't want to hear about them," said Senator Prish, who up to this time had been quietly drawing pictures on a pad. "What else did you find?"

"We discovered some remarkable wind velocities and some extraordinary temperatures," said Byrd. "We brought back, indeed, hundreds of thousands of interesting figures. Our physicist took gradients of the snow. His findings are, I think, extremely valuable."

"Did he get these valuable gradients back safely?" asked Senator Vanfield.

"Oh, yes," said Byrd.

"Well, would you say they had a value comparable to that of—ah—radium, maybe?"

"A gradient," said Byrd, a little wearily, "is a rational integral homogeneous isobaric function of a number of quantics. I am sure you gentlemen will not be disappointed in them."

"They sound splendid," said Senator Prish. Another long pause ensued.

"We got the contour of the ocean, too—with the sonic depth-finder," said Byrd, proudly. "The contour of the ocean had never been got before."

"A fine achievement," said Senator Vanfield.

"Thank you," said Byrd. "We found some very deep spots." Everybody fell silent.

"There's no way at all of getting at this coal, you say?" asked Senator Grosbeak.

"No," Senator Eakin told him.

"Well, how about oil?" asked Senator Grosbeak. The others stirred uneasily.

"We covered that," said Eakin. This time there was a very long pause.

"There's a great deal more work to be done down there," said Byrd, "I'm going back again, of course."

"Ah—yes, that's quite right," said Senator Vanfield, "and splendid too. But if I were you I wouldn't claim any more land. I think we have enough land now. I don't want you to overwork yourself."

"Well, he might claim some just a little less icy, if there is any," said Senator Grosbeak. "Is there?"

"It's all a lost, dead, enormously fascinating wilderness of ice, the empire of the winds, the forlorn frontier of adventure, the farthest south of the Stars and Stripes," said Byrd.

"Well, I wouldn't claim any more of it," said Senator Grosbeak. "I guess, gentlemen," he added, "that's all we wanted to know. Let us adjourn—and thank you, Admiral Byrd." They got up and shook hands with the explorer. Then they all filed quietly out of the committee room—except Senator Prish. He was still drawing pictures on a pad, shading in little circles and squares and gradients.

Thoughts from Mr. Tierney

Last Monday, when I was just sitting around, without a constructive or helpful thought in my head, up popped a communication from my representative in Congress, the Hon. William L. Tierney, like myself an old Connecticutian of fine family. If it hadn't been for his speech (it was a speech he sent me), I should have spent the day flipping over the pages of a photoplay magazine and leering at the pictures of the lady stars. Mr. Tierney's speech, however, gave me something to think about and also stirred up an idea or two of my own which may be of help to Mr. Tierney and to Congress and indirectly to the millions of Americans whose happiness, the gentleman from Connecticut points out, is handicapped by paralysis. Epilepsy, I would say, but then Mr. Tierney is probably in closer touch with happiness than I am.

Mr. Tierney's speech is the first speech I have read in a long time. Ordinarily, I pay no attention to what goes on in Congress until one of the representatives calls another one a cockeyed so-and-so and the two

Editor's Note: William Laurence Tierney, a Connecticut attorney, served as a senator in the 72nd Congress, 1931–33.

go for each other right on the floor. That, it seems to me, is something. Speeches, as a rule, are nothing. Mr. Tierney's, however, has a number of interesting points. It takes only about fifteen minutes to read and he gets immediately into what he has to say without any preamble. He starts right off: "Mr. Chairman, I desire to make a few observations in support of the Reconstruction Finance Corporation bill now reported out of my committee on Banking and Currency under the new title of a Bill to Provide Financial Facilities for Financial Institutions to Aid in Financing Agriculture, Commerce, and Industry, and for Other Purposes."

Here was something which I saw at a glance it was my duty as a citizen to Grasp. It gave me the guilty realization that for months I have been letting finance bills go along without even knowing that their titles had been changed. That kind of laxity is bound to let a citizen in for trouble. Imagine, at a dinner party, saying something to the lovely lady on your right about the Reconstruction Finance Corporation bill only to have her come back, after a peal of cold and silvery laughter, with the withering question "Are you perhaps trying to say the Bill to Provide Financial Facilities for Financial Institutions to Aid in Financing Agriculture, Commerce, and Industry, and for Other Purposes?" *You* might weather such a withering, but I couldn't, for when I am embarrassed at dinner parties the front of my shirt begins to rise and when I push it down it goes plop and comes right up again, with the result that I have to hold it down with both hands and thus get nothing to eat.

The body of Mr. Tierney's speech was rather depressing for Monday reading but as a citizen I felt I ought to go ahead with it. It was mostly about the bad shape everything is in, particularly the banks. Mr. Tierney pointed out that the banks are under stress and peril owing to war conditions. "While not at war," he said, "our financial institutions are under a like pressure and peril. In effect, we are at war." This reasoning, while colorful, is, it seems to me, misleading and likely to cause people to enlist, to kiss each other goodbye, to compose march songs, and to go around bragging that they won the Depression. I don't see that any good can come from twisting things around so that it appears the banks have got us into war. It would have been simpler and more convincing to get up a swell simile about banks and ships, because after all they both go down in much the same way, with treasure on board, and are not heard of again except possibly as derelicts drifting around a lonely sea or standing empty and forlorn at the corner of Fifth Avenue and some cross-street. Had my representative taken this slant he could have touched on another idea which the bank-ship simile calls up: that is, why doesn't the president of a bank go down with his bank, the way a skipper goes down with his ship? Certainly, there is nothing one can think of that a bank president could do if he didn't have a bank. He could ride a horse in Central Park for a while, but not forever. He could sit around his club forever, of course, but that would be mortifying, with nobody to order around but waiters. It would be much better for him simply to go down with his bank. Of course it would be harder, in a way, for a banker to go down with his bank than for a captain to go down with his ship, for, when a bank closes, the bank building itself is at the disadvantage of still being where it was. In this connection, I would offer the suggestion that when a bank closes and all the clerks and tellers and vice-presidents leave and the light and heat is turned off and the charwomen come no more to fill the watercoolers, the president just stay in the old abandoned building alone. This would give the city something of the fascination and mystery of the sea. It would build up legends (and we need legends). For years it would be rumored, say, that President Hotchkiss K. Zegafeld, of the Thirty-first National, who went down with his bank in 1929, was still to be seen on moonlit nights prowling around the inside of the old building. He would become known as the Prowling Dutchman and mothers would hush their children to sleep with tales of his eerie flittings about in the tellers' cages.

This, however, is getting pretty far away from Mr. Tierney's speech, in which, on page 3, he says what seems to me another unfortunate thing: namely, that about a billion dollars in currency is now out of circulation and *between the mattresses.* A billion dollars tucked away under the bedclothes of the nation! What kind of tip is that to give to the desperately hard-up citizens of this country? It is one thing to spend years and years becoming a fake butler in order to get at the drawing-room safe—only your inveterate criminal does that—but it is another to pop into a bedroom, pull up the mattress, and get away with a roll of bills. Anybody could do that, and thousands of people probably will. Mark my words, Tierney, that tip of yours is going to lead to a wave of second-story work, sending of mysterious theatre tickets to get people away from home, catcalling and cries for help in the backyard to get people out of bed, fake fires, bedroom farces, and pernicious harlequinade generally.

One thing in Mr. Tierney's speech—toward the end—is calculated to give me hope in case I ever want to run for Congress. I can never remember names or faces, a misfortune which is intensified by the fact that I am always sure I have met everybody I see. Mr. Tierney shows that weakness of memory about names is negligible in Congress. In referring to an eminent gentleman who testified in a Senate hearing, he says he thinks it was either Mr. Ecker, president of the Metropolitan Life Insurance Company, or Mr. Morgan Brainard, president of the Aetna Insurance Company, of Hartford. If that's as close as you have to come, we could be a Congressman right now. Of course this uncertainty of Mr. Tierney's, while comforting to a would-be Congressman, is rather disconcerting to an earnest-minded constituent, trying to find out what conditions really are. Maybe, for example, the billion dollars isn't under the mattress after all but behind the print of Rosa Bonheur's "The Horse Fair" in the front hall. I can't be ransacking the whole house.

$\mathscr{P}$OLO IN THE HOME

THE ADAPTATION OF THE GAME OF POLO TO THE HOME, or apartment, would seem, on first thought, out of the question. But no sport is worthwhile and no progress possible if the player is not willing and eager to be at some pains to overcome obstacles. It will be said, first of all, that the house is no place for a horse, particularly a highly strung animal such as the polo pony invariably is. Naturally, one cannot take a horse directly into a room and begin riding him to polo balls. He should first be led, slowly, several times, through that portion of the house which is to serve as the playing floor, and allowed to familiarize himself with the little nooks and corners, the doorways and closets. A quivering bright-eyed horse backed suddenly, during the height of play, into a bathroom which he has never seen before, is quite likely to become so frightened by the shining nickel work and the glistening tub that he may get alto-gether out of hand. This strangeness would soon wear off, however, with a little care and foresight. Wear and tear on the home must be considered, of course, but how simple to remove all breakable furniture and to pad the heavier pieces that cannot readily be shifted. A thick, durable floor cloth is also recommended and some form of stout wire netting to protect windows, wall brackets, and chandeliers from mallets and hooves. The present season's consistent weekend rain has proved that outdoor polo is a slave to circumstance. Indoor polo, in armories and the like, serves a limited purpose, but lacks the intimate charm of polo in one's own home. In low-ceilinged apartments, play is inclined to be awkward and unless the ceiling can be removed without embarrassment, it is better not to play.

A country estate, or large town house, is of course the ideal grounds, but the small apartment will be found adaptable if one is careful to choose up sides of two, rather than four. Eight horses in the parlor, bedroom, and bath arrangement are altogether too many.

The game of parlor polo will be a boon to many a virile host who suddenly finds his guests producing pencils and himself, before long, passing around paper for another four or five rounds of Guggenheim or "Where does a penguin keep his ears?"

"What do you say I go and fetch the ponies?" boomed in a bluff, hearty voice by the host, is almost sure to set the less undesirable elements of a party to looking at their wristwatches, and, with the advent of the animals, the evening is certain to be left to those vigorous souls who make an evening worthwhile.

"*Think of it, Madam! I was only sixteen at the time.*"

"*And* I *say he* couldn't *have hypnotized you!*"

*"For instance, Doctor, sometimes I feel as if I were travelling
at a speed of more than two hundred miles an hour."*

"I have a neurosis."

"*While you were out of the room I lost my mind.*"

*"Then I get this feeling that my feet are trying to
tell me something but can't."*

"You and your suppressed desires!"

*"You've taken the best years of my life, that's *what you've done!*"*

"*A subtle change has come over my wife, Doctor.*"

*"Don't you think the subconscious has been done to death
and that it's high time someone rediscovered the conscious?"*

"You bring out the worst in me—the most feminine."

No Sex After the First of the Year

WHITE AND I BELIEVE THAT THERE WILL BE NO SEX after the first of the year, which is why we wanted the book brought out. Everything points to that. America never quite knew what to do with sex, you see, not being able to grasp it clearly. Instead of being, say, a charming little bibelot, which it is to the French, it got to be more like a rubber plant around the house, large and cumbersome and more or less outmoded, outmoded because we have got a little tired of sex since the war when, as a matter of fact, it was first openly recognized in this country, and faced squarely. Of course, we faced it too squarely.

I should say that Americans work too hard and play too hard for sex to have a fair chance to exist much after the first of the year. It is, of course, neither work nor play, but something in between, which we have never thoroughly grasped, as I say. Any more than we have grasped drink. We don't know how to drink. One comes finally to have a high disdain for things he doesn't understand, which is why there was this great wave of prohibition to get rid of something we didn't really understand. The same is going to be true of sex.

One detects that, I think, by observing, as we point out in the book, the substitutes that are gradually taking the place of sex. I mean the great

Editor's Note: *Is Sex Necessary? Or Why You Feel the Way You Do*, by James Thurber and E. B. White, with illustrations by James Thurber, appeared in 1929. This was Thurber's first book, and it was published to considerable acclaim.

interest in games, anagrams, yo-yo, puzzles, football, etc., etc. In a year or two, therefore, any novel that is primarily concerned with sex as a motivating force will be ridiculous and distorting. Sex, of course, always will be there, in people's lives, but it will never be the same old absorbing interest; it will assume an importance of about the same kind as the Rothstein case, something that is always with one, that there is considerable talk about, but which really has no force at all as a factor in anyone's life.

Of course sex, as we know it—in America—was brought to its highest state of development, interest, and excitement by the younger generation. There was only one original younger generation, that which came into being during and just after the war. But the members of that generation, that genuine younger generation, are finding gray in their hair; they can no longer stay up after 2:00 A.M. and feel well the next morning; they are getting quietly and respectably married; most of them indeed are married and have children.

The great momentum that they gave to sex has therefore slowed down, and sex finds itself in the situation of a plane which can maintain itself in the air only at a speed of a hundred miles an hour; it is now travelling around sixty miles an hour, and is bound to crash, about January 1st.

Editor's Note: Millionaire gambler Arnold Rothstein, also known as Mr. Big, reigned for twenty years in the Manhattan underworld, fencing bonds, financing speakeasies, "fixing" nearly anything, including the 1919 World Series. According to the papers of the time, he owned Broadway and most of Manhattan, though no indictment ever stuck to him. He died in a poker game in 1928.

$\mathcal{T}$HE STORY OF THE BICYCLE

Fig. 1
Early Woman

ALTHOUGH THE BICYCLE HAS NOT MULTIPLIED anywhere near as rapidly as the rabbit, it must be borne in mind that in the beginning there was only one bicycle whereas there were two rabbits. It is perhaps unfortunate that both the vehicle and the animal are just about the same today as they were to begin with. They have not reached a very high point of development; they are not, as a matter of fact, really Getting Anywhere. This, to be sure, is also true of the bugle, the beagle, the button, and practically everything else. Indeed, one of the few things I can think of at the moment which have really made appreciable progress is Woman. (See Figs. 1 and 2). However, we are getting off the subject, for this lecture is to be concerned solely with the origin and progress, such as it has been, of the wheel. I am sorry, but that is what it is to be concerned with. Next month, if you are good little boys and girls, I shall tell you something more about Woman.

The first wheel constructed by the hand of man was square. This played hell with the early chari-oteers, who were jiggled and jerked and bumped about during races and battles like so many jumping jacks in a windstorm.

Fig. 2
Modern
Woman

Acutely uncomfortable as it was, this type of wheel was used for several centuries, until, in fact, the year 247 B.C., when a Greek named Thycides, by cutting off each point of the square wheel, brought into existence the octagonal wheel. This was something of an improvement, but not much, for as one famous charioteer of the period observed, "Maybe she don't jolt you as high as she once did, but she jolts you twice as often." The truth of this observation becomes immediately apparent when you study Figs. 4 and 5. (Fig. 3 has been lost.)

When Thycides had fitted the new octagonal wheels to his chariot, he called to his wife to come out and see what the genius of Man had brought to pass. She went out and looked. "Now we're getting somewheres!" cried Thycides, as he jolted around the backyard. "Are we?" said his wife, coldly, and she went back to cleaning the silver. Undaunted, Thycides went round and round and as the oc-

Fig. 5. tagonal wheels turned and turned their edges gradually wore smooth and the round wheel as we know it today came into existence (Fig. 6). (Fig. 6 has also disappeared.)

In the centuries that followed, mankind adjusted round wheels to the cart, the wagon, the dray, the buckboard, the phaeton, the surrey, the stagecoach, and the horsecar. It did not, however, occur to the human being until 1871 that a thing with only two wheels, one in front of the other, could be made to stay upright while you were on it. The idea had never crossed Archimedes' mind, and Galileo was always too busy with something else. It finally remained for Charles Bekkel, the inventor of the two-wheeled bicycle, to demonstrate the fact that if you rode 'er fast enough and didn't jiggle 'er too much, she would stay upright. Like Thycides before him, he shouted to his wife to come and witness what he, with the help of the Almighty, had figured out. She went out into the dooryard. "I can ride on two wheels, Maude!" cried Bekkel. "Lookit, I can ride on two wheels!" His wife viewed the noisy proceedings briefly. "Remember you got your Sunday pants on," she said, and went back to her Mason jars.

Fig. 4.

In 1884 there were only seventeen bicycles in

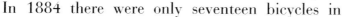

Washington, D.C. When this is compared to the figures for 1894, which I have unfortunately mislaid, it will be seen, or would be if we had the figures, that the increase had been remarkable. The increase continued to be remarkable in the United States until 1904, when suddenly there was a terrific drop. America had discovered sex. The whole country immediately lost interest in the bicycle and began to play pillow, Post Office, footy-footy, and house. Today there are not more than sixty-five hundred bicycles in New York State, or in the country at large, I can't remember which. And what was the rabbit doing all this time? Let us take a peep and see. In the past seventy years the total number of bicycles in the world has lagged far behind the total number of rabbits. There is considerable room for doubt as to whether, short of a rabbit purge, or a bicycle boom, or both, the two figures will ever reach a parity. In Australia alone there are more than 75,569,132 rabbits. Some of you may find it interesting to compare this figure with the numbers one frequently sees on the sides of New York Central freight cars.

The highest number that I personally have ever encountered on a freight car was 56798720483342. This is exactly 15,347 times as large as the total number of bicycles that have been manufactured in the entire world since the installation of the first official U.S. government Weather Bureau (March 3, 1839). That bureau, we might notice in passing, was set up by one John R. Strobe, in Fond du Lac (Bottom of the Lake), Wis. (Wisconsin). Strobe, possibly as a result of his long years of solitude in his hut at the farthest point of Cape Gleason, took to playing nine men's morris with a bottle full of fireflies, and had to be replaced in 1857.

A question which is frequently asked of me takes this form: "Is the bicycle here to stay?" It is difficult to say. We all know, of course, that in the past thirty years the bicycle has taken a pretty bad tossing around from the automobile and from certain low-flying airplanes. There is probably no more upsetting experience in the world than to be "clipped" by the wing of an airplane as you cycle idly along some lovely old country road whose hedges are sweet with eglantine. Nobody can safely predict anything—although everybody I know spends most of his time predicting everything—but I should like to hazard the guess that if this clipping continues at its present rate everybody with any brains at all will give up the bicycle and take to the woods on foot.

This inevitably brings us to the question of how many people there are with any brains at all. My own investigations have resulted in some rather depressing findings. They show, among other things, that 17 percent of the male population of the world cool their porridge with their hats, and that 87 percent of all women throw a baseball with their right foot advanced. Moreover, seven persons out of every ten believe that the common toad causes warts and this in spite of the fact that it has a precious jewel in its head! Many of my findings are too disconcerting to go into.

If you will all quit rustling your programs and sit still for a moment, I shall tell you, in closing, the ill-fated story of Charles R. Butterost. Butterost, who for forty-five years had ridden bicycles, kiddy-kars, taxi-cabs, and airplanes, without feeling that any of them had really got him anywhere, one afternoon climbed into a baby carriage at the top of a hill, pulled the pink coverlet up to his chin, started her down the hill at a breakneck pace, and shot himself through the head as he went.

I am not recommending this as a way out, I am just telling you.

HELP! HELP! ANOTHER CLASSIFICATIONIZATION

Now a certain Public Health expert has come up with a new classification of me and my age group, or, to be precise, those of us who are in our sixties or older. The Public Healthist divides us into the institutionalized and the noninstitutionalized. As good luck, prayer, and a sound diet would have it, I belong to the noninstitutionalized, which includes the working, the up and about but unemployed, and those who are just lying in bed at home. When the time comes for me to be committed to the funny house or a nursing home, I will become an ex-noninstitutionalized person. If and when, upon good behavior, I shall be released in the custody of my family, my designation will then be that of an unex-noninstitutionalized person. When I am put back in, after raising hell on Third Avenue, breaking up Nixon rallies, and other subversive conduct, my new tag will be, as any modern child could tell you at a glance, "re-unex-noninstitutionalized."

I do not propose to take it lying down when I am dragged back to the institution, and I have a plan already worked out to plague the Public Health expert in charge till Hell won't have it. I will pretend to be a maximum bed-rest case until my chart is filled with overconfident de-

scriptions of my various inabilities. Then one bright day, when the Healthist makes his rounds, I will be hanging from the chandelier in my room,
not by my neck but by my heels, and reciting, without missing a word
or rhyme, all of *The Prisoner of Chillon*. I like to think that the Healthist
will have a number of journalists, colleagues, and state officials in tow,
perhaps even the Governor. I like to think of him being so shattered by
the failure of his analyses and prognosticationization of my case that he
will have to be completely reclassified himself. Oh, I shall be able to
handle him, have no fear of that.

"Come, come, Mr. Turble," he will say, with a firmness showing
clear signs of crumble, "be a good statistic, now, for these gentlemen.
And shake hands with the Governor."

"If the Governor wishes to shake hands with me," I'll reply, "he will
have to lie down on his back. I intend to hang here until I have finished
'Intimations of Immortality.'" It will be a great, if considerably confused,
victory for me.

I had planned to veer off here into one of my attacks on the Iza-
tionizers, who have deformed and bloated our language by izationizing
almost every noun and adjective ending in "al," but I have decided to
conserve my strength for that triumphant day in the funny house or the
nursing home. However, I have enough strength for one crack in conclusion. The public figures in America, who are largely responsible for
the beating English has taken, and is still taking, don't seem to realize
that they are playing verbally into the hands of the Communists. Nothing
reduces the shape, color, and vitality of individuality so much as izationizing people into a colorless lump of category. I have viewed with
alarm, this many a year, the decline of the spoken word. The trend toward
massive meaninglessness got its greatest boost, if you haven't caught my
alarms in the past, during the McCarthage period, when there seemed to
be an unspoken slogan, incidental to the attack on everything all along
the line. The slogan was *lingua delenda est*. I fell asleep upon this ominous
Latin phrase recently, and dreamed a nightmare. I may be overexerting
myself, but I am going to tell what it was anyway.

Two men in uniforms were measuring me for a uniform just like
theirs. One man had no mouth and the other one had no ears, and their

names, displayed on badges, were Tweedledumb and Tweedledeaf. When they got me dressed up in a kind of gray straitjacket, Tweedledeaf said, "It makes you look like everybody else. Does it make you feel like everybody else?"

"Yes," I said. "How am I going to tell myself from me?" Tweedledeaf grinned evilly. "I can't hear what you're saying," he said, "but Tweedledumb can. If you want any information, ask him."

I was about to protest that Tweedledumb couldn't say anything, but I realized it wouldn't do any good, whatever I said. "An amusing thought has just struck me," said Tweedledeaf. "You may not be able to tell yourself from you, since you look like everybody, and everybody looks like everybody else, so I will put a tail on you." And he put a tail on me, a big chesty tail in a dark suit, whose derby kept going up and down his forehead as he slowly chewed something. I woke up at that point, yelling, as usual. I have put down this little description not so much to amuse or frighten anybody as to have a record of it in case my memory should succumb to the obliterating processes of age. Right now, it is all right. Right now my classificationization chart reads as follows: "Sex, male. Age, going on sixty-two. Color of moods, grayish black. Height, indeterminate because of ducking. Occupation, sympathizer with lost or unpopular causes. Social status (subject to change without notice), noninstitutionalized.

I'll see you in the funny house.

"I'm the termite man."

MORE OR LESS RELATED TO THE SELF-PERCEPTIONS OF MEN AND WOMEN

"Sir, you are speaking of the woman I once loved!"

"Now take you and me, Blodgett—we're both men of the world."

"Dr. Rathbone told her she was disingenuous and she's been acting that way ever since."

"Her maid told ours that she has a heart tattooed on her hip."

"I'm warning you now, Papa!"

"*Papa spank if you muss up his handkerchiefs.*"

"Sober, Mrs. Tomkins is the personification of virtue."

"Some people glow inside when they're happy, but I buzz."

"My husband has insured my life for a hundred thousand dollars.
Isn't that sweet?"

LOOK OUT FOR THE WARELIANS!

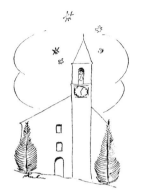

IT HAS BEEN A LONG TIME SINCE ORSON WELLES SCARED everybody to death, but the invasion of the Martians is still a live subject. Thousands of people in Ohio and Louisiana have not yet come out of hiding, pastors and editorial writers still allude to the Advent of the Little Men, and for months to come comedians will bound into cocktail parties making awful faces and shouting, "We got you, you miserable Earth Creatures!" But what gives last year's invasion of New Jersey a new and special timeliness is the astronomical fact that in August or September of this year, 1939, Mars and Earth will be closer to each other than they have been for fifteen years. The two planets, which are usually quite far apart, come within striking distance of each other (35,000,000 miles) every fifteen or seventeen years. The last time this happened was in 1924. Late this summer there will be another Opposition near Perihelion.

Because of the coming conjunction, I have been doing a little research on the interesting problem of interplanetary communication, with the aid of some books on astronomy and a powerful telescope an aunt gave me for Christmas. Sometimes I put down the books and the telescope and just think. In this way I have arrived at what I call Conclusion A. This may be stated much more clearly than you might expect. Conclusion A

Editor's Note: On October 30, 1938, *Orson Welles's Mercury Theater on the Air* broadcast an adaptation of H. G. Wells's *The War of the Worlds*. The "on-the-spot" news coverage reported an invasion of New Jersey by Martians, causing widespread panic; many people fled their homes, and others were hospitalized for shock.

assumes, quite simply, that the inhabitants of the three planets nearest to us, Mars, Venus, and Mercury, are approximately seventeen times as scared of us as we are of them.

I am going to leave the Outer Planets out of this discussion because they are too far away to be in any danger from us. Jupiter, the nearest of these Outer, or Safer, Planets, is some 300,000,000 miles farther away from the sun than we are, and Neptune is almost six times as far away as Jupiter. They are sitting very pretty and they probably know it. An airplane averaging 390 miles an hour would take 114 years to get to Jupiter and obviously none of the Little Men from Earth who set out in one would be alive when the plane landed. The Inner, or Imperilled, Planets, however, are not so well off as Jupiter and Neptune. They are, or at least they think they are, in desperate and imminent danger of an invasion by Warel. "Warel" is my idea of the kind of name the other terrestrial planets must have for Earth; it is made up of the words "war" and "cruel" and for the purposes of this study (or for any other purpose) is a much better term for our planet than the one we use.

Two of the Imperilled Planets, Mars and Venus, have a general similarity to Earth, which has caused astronomers to assume that they may be inhabited. Mercury is rather similar to Earth, too, but I guess we can leave her out of this. Mercury presents always only one hemisphere to the sun and if there were any people on that burning side they would be too miserable to devise any deviltry or to be afraid of anything except the sun. (Mercury is three times as close to the sun as we are.) Any beings who might exist on the hemisphere that is constantly turned away from the sun would be 237 times colder than the Eskimos and nobody could be that cold and get away with it. I think we can safely conclude, then, that there isn't anybody at all on Mercury, either for us to worry about or to be worried about us. Let us fix our telescope on Mars and Venus.

Because of certain physical phenomena, Mars and Venus are not nearly so well adapted as we are to the development of that Higher Intelligence which has made the Earth Creatures, or Warelians, what they are today. The atmosphere on Venus is much too thick and that on Mars far too rarefied to produce the intelligent human being as we know him. The inhabitants of Venus live in a kind of overcharged aqueous fog and are slow of thought and sluggish of movement. This kind of atmosphere fosters the development of a rather stupid, kindly people who do not go in for weapons of war other than the club and the brickbat. It is extremely unlikely that the Venusians possess anything made of steel or want to possess anything made of steel. The heaviness of the atmosphere, the scarcity of oxygen, and the prevalence of carbon dioxide make Venus a dreamy kind of planet with no genius at all in the arts of hellishness. We can put Venus down as a friendly planet; friendly but frightened.

Mars, as I have said, has a thin atmosphere,* and you know what that does to you. The Martians can't hear very well, they are constantly swallowing, and they are always slightly dizzy. A great many of them find it difficult to keep anything on their stomachs. The Martians are afflicted with torpor and indecision in certain seasons and a vague melancholy in all seasons. I think we may assume that in implements of warfare they have not got beyond the slingshot era and that they have no desire to. Martians are canal workers and there are so many millions of miles of canals on Mars that the Martians have no time for anything else, even if they could think of anything else. They get up and work on the canals and they go to bed and get up and work on the canals again. Like the Venusians, they have a great deal of carbon dioxide, but a great deal of carbon dioxide does not get a planet anywhere. My researches have established the probability that Mars also has hornblende and gneiss, but I can find no traces of steel, oil, warships, battle planes, speakers' platforms, national flags, or anything else. Martians may be a trifle more active than Venusians, but they are not warlike; they are sad and they want to be left alone. The inhabitants of both these planets put together would not have the energy or spirit to invade Halley's Comet even if it came to a stop and cooled off. They have not yet developed a Higher Intelligence. If we fix the intelligence of the Warelians at 1 (and after

---

* Webster's International Dictionary for 1927 says that Mars has an "exceedingly rare atmosphere—perhaps like that surrounding the summits of the Himalayas." The more recent Websters don't mention the Himalayas. Martian air has apparently become so thin in the past ten years that there is nothing on Earth to compare it to.

what happened on Earth last October that is putting it high), the intelligence of the Martians and the Venusians may be fairly represented by
the symbol −17. Now, the more intelligent you are, in a planetary sense,
the less scared you are going to be, in an interplanetary sense. Let us
take a peek at the Intelligence Quotient of the Warelian as indicated by
his Fear Level. This will give us some idea of how dumb and how frightened Mars and Venus must be.

None of the hundreds of thousands of Warelians who were planet-
struck on that great day last October were smart enough to realize that
even when Mars is closest to us (35,000,000 miles) it would take Martian
planes travelling at 200 miles per hour twenty years to reach New Jersey.
(I am leaving out the problem of stocking the planes with food and fuel,
even though this is an important consideration, because of the fact that
the Martians probably have no fuel.) A Martian warrior who was thirty-
two years old when he set out to invade Earth would be in his fifties
when he landed, even if everything went all right during the trip; a normal
amount of engine trouble would hold him up until he was in his sixties.
It doesn't require any more brain than a resident of Neptune has to figure
out the unsurmountable rigors of the trip. A man who spent two decades
hurtling through space would be airsick and Space Drunk and very likely
a pitiable sight to behold on account of Speed Bends, Comet Shock,
Stratosphere Burn, Sky Eye, and Star Deafness. A child on Jupiter would
know that an aging Martian arriving cross and sick after a trying twenty-
year trip would not be in any shape to go around killing Americans.

Now, if we Warelians are too ignorant to have figured out the impossibility of an invasion from Mars, how much less likely is it that the
Martians have figured out the impossibility of an invasion from Earth?
About seventeen times less likely, we find in referring back to the Martian
intelligence symbol. Thus, since intelligence and fear move in identical
orbits, the Martians are seventeen times as scared as we are. They think
Earth is only a few thousand miles away. A Martian at his best can barely
put two and two together and he would never be able to comprehend a
figure as large as 35,000,000. All a Martian really knows about us is that

there we are in the skies, looking near and ominous at all times and very near and very ominous in August and September of certain years. The Martians were intensely frightened by the close approach of Warel in 1924, 1909, 1892, and 1877. In 1877 millions of them gathered in their primitive caves and prayed their primitive prayers. Hundreds of thousands of them killed themselves and many others went crazy or fled into the woods of Syrtis Major. I wish I could let the Martians know that there is really no danger, that we are never going to drop down on them through space. Only one little thought cheers me up when I think about the Martians and how scared they are of Warel. Martians haven't got a strong enough intelligence or a vivid enough imagination to picture what the Little Men of Earth are really like. That's why, with all their melancholy and all their dizziness and all their tedious work on the canals, they are a happier people than we are. We know exactly how horrible and terrifying the Little Men of Earth actually are. It isn't a pleasant thing to know.

MAME THURBER'S NEVER-FAIL DEVIL'S FOOD CAKE, WITH $100 CHOCOLATE FROSTING

THE FOLLOWING RECIPE WAS SUBMITTED BY JAMES Thurber to the Columbus *Dispatch* Cooking School, held at the Palace Theatre in May 1951.

"At eighty-five, my mother (Mrs. Charles Thurber, Southern Hotel) is still planning a cookbook of her own. She was a famous pastry cook and maker of chocolate candy. Her candy was considered the finest made by any amateur in the country, but her devil's food cake is a professional masterpiece. To make a great cake you have to have a light hand. My mother still has that. Best wishes to you and to the cooking project."

NEVER-FAIL DEVIL'S FOOD CAKE

1 cup light brown sugar
½ cup unsweetened chocolate, finely grated
½ cup milk
1 egg yolk

Combine and cook together over low heat until mixture is smooth. Cool slightly while mixing other ingredients.

½ cup butter
1 cup light brown sugar
2 eggs, separated
½ cup milk
2½ cups sifted cake flour
¼ teaspoon baking powder
½ teaspoon salt
1 teaspoon vanilla
1 teaspoon soda

Cream together butter and sugar. Beat in yolks. Add milk alternately with sifted flour, baking powder, baking soda, and salt. Stir in cooled chocolate mixture and vanilla. Gently fold in stiffly beaten egg whites. Pour into 2 greased 8-inch square cake pans. Bake in a 350°F. oven for 30 to 35 minutes, or until done.

$100 CHOCOLATE FROSTING

¼ pound butter
1 square unsweetened chocolate, melted
⅔ pound confectioners' sugar
1 egg
1 teaspoon vanilla
1 teaspoon lemon juice
½ cup chopped nuts

Melt butter; cool. Add with melted chocolate and confectioners' sugar to beaten egg. Stir in vanilla and lemon juice. Beat until smooth. Fold in nuts. Frosts one 8-inch layer cake.

ʃOURCES

Drawings

Endpapers: *The New Yorker*, December 10, 1932.
Frontispiece: Ad for Bergdorf Goodman, *The New York Times*, January 21, 1940.
Title page: *The New Yorker*, April 4, 1936.
Page vii *Williams Record*, April 13, 1940.
 ix: *Newark Call*, July 4, 1936; carried in AP story that ran several places.
 xi: Unpublished.
 1: Cover, *The New Yorker*, February 29, 1936.
 3: *The New Yorker*, July 18, 1942.
 8: *Waterbury* (Conn.) *Republican*, January 29, 1939.
 9: *The New Yorker*, April 28, 1934.
 10: Official program, O.S.U. vs. Northwestern, October 23, 1937.
 11: Official program, O.S.U. vs. Michigan, November 19, 1937; reprinted in the *Sun Dial*, May 7, 1941, captioned.
 12: Ad for French Line cruises, *The New Yorker*, January 6, 1934.
 13: Ad for French Line cruises, *The New Yorker*, May 6, 1933.
 14: Adapted from a cover, *The New Yorker*, February 9, 1936.
 16: *The New Yorker*, March 14, 1942.
 22: *The New Yorker*, January 25, 1941.
 23: *The New Yorker*, October 13, 1945.
 24: *The New Yorker*, July 15, 1939.
 25: *The New Yorker*, October 20, 1945.
 26: *The New Yorker*, September 21, 1935.

Page 29: Ad for French Line cruises, *The New Yorker*, January 14, 1933.

32: *The New Yorker*, November 18, 1944.

35: Illustration from "Letter from the States," *Bermudian*, February 1950.

37: Illustration for "If You Ask Me," *PM*, October 10, 1944.

39: Illustration for "If You Ask Me," *PM*, February 24, 1941.

43: Illustration from "Letter from the States," *Bermudian*, May 1950.

45: Illustration for "Impressions of a First Lady," *Stage*, March, 1936.

47: *The New Yorker*, February 23, 1935.

48: *The New Yorker*, March 9, 1935.

49: *The New Yorker*, April 8, 1933.

50: *Saturday Review*, March 13, 1937.

51: *The New Yorker*, November 12, 1932.

52: *Sun Dial*, April 24, 1940.

53: *The New Yorker*, January 19, 1935.

54: *The New Yorker*, March 21, 1936.

55: Unpublished.

56: *The New Yorker*, December 1, 1934.

57: *The New Yorker*, December 16, 1933.

58: *The New Yorker*, September 22, 1945.

59: *The New Yorker*, November 20, 1943.

60: *The New Yorker*, March 30, 1935.

61: *The New Yorker*, May 26, 1934.

62: *The New Yorker*, February 22, 1936.

63: *The New Yorker*, June 19, 1937.

64: *The New Yorker*, July 3, 1937.

65: *The New Yorker*, February 29, 1936. Thurber's earlier caption, which appears on the original drawing, reads: "If they never found the husband's body could they do anything to the wife?"

66: *The New Yorker*, December 10, 1938.

67: "Marriages Are Made in Heaven," unpublished.

68: "Divorces Are Okay in Hell," unpublished.

69: *The New Yorker*, May 23, 1936.

70: *The New Yorker*, December 12, 1931.

71: *The New Yorker*, October 20, 1934.

72: *The New Yorker*, December 22, 1934.

73: *The New Yorker*, July 10, 1943.

74: *The New Yorker*, September 11, 1943.

75: *The New Yorker*, January 11, 1936.

76: *The New Yorker*, August 13, 1932.

77: Ad for S. N. Behrman's *Rain from Heaven*, *The New Yorker*, February 2, 1935.

79: Cover, *The New Yorker*, April 29, 1939.

81: *The New Yorker*, January 14, 1939.

85: *The New Yorker*, January 14, 1933.

89: *The New Yorker*, October 8, 1932.

90: *The New Yorker*, June 1, 1935.

91: *The New Yorker*, August 12, 1939.

92: *The New Yorker*, November 5, 1932.

93: *The New Yorker*, September 3, 1932.

94: *The New Yorker*, March 5, 1938.

95: *The New Yorker*, September 16, 1944.

96: *The New Yorker*, April 24, 1937.

97: *The New Yorker*, November 4, 1933.

98: *Detroit Free Press Sunday Magazine*, February 25, 1940.

99: Cover, *Sports Illustrated*, November 6, 1960.

100: *The New Yorker*, September 29, 1934.

101: *The New Yorker*, September 5, 1936.

102: *The New Yorker*, February 19, 1938.

103: *The New Yorker*, April 4, 1936.

108: *The New Yorker*, November 28, 1936.

109: Ad for French Line cruises, *The New Yorker*, November 18, 1933.

113: *The New Yorker*, January 13, 1934. Originally run with the caption: "I'm bored to tears with Sistie Dall."

117: *The New Yorker*, October 2, 1937.

119: Ad for Fisher Body, *The New Yorker*, September 23, 1933.

121: *The New Yorker*, December 8, 1934.

122: *The New Yorker*, April 13, 1935.

123: *The New Yorker*, December 14, 1935.

124: *The New Yorker*, February 15, 1941.

125: *The New Yorker*, May 12, 1934.

126: *The New Yorker*, September 24, 1932.

127: *The New Yorker*, January 16, 1932.

128: *The New Yorker*, March 23, 1935.

129: *The New Yorker*, October 16, 1937.

130: Ad for S. N. Behrman's *Rain from Heaven*, *The New Yorker*, January 26, 1935.

131: Ad for S. N. Behrman's *Rain from Heaven*, *The New Yorker*, February 9, 1935.

133: *The New Yorker*, May 3, 1941.

139: *The New Yorker*, December 5, 1936.

141: Ad for Fisher Body, *The New Yorker*, November 18, 1933.

142: *Detroit Free Press Sunday Magazine*, February 25, 1940.

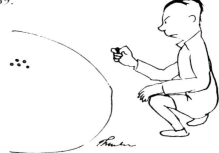

Page 143: *The New Yorker*, September 3, 1944.
    144: *The New Yorker*, June 24, 1939.
    145: *The New Yorker*, May 8, 1937.
    146: *The New Yorker*, April 25, 1936.
    147: *The New Yorker*, October 7, 1933.
    148: *The New Yorker*, January 9, 1932.
    149: *The New Yorker*, April 20, 1940.
    150: *The New Yorker*, July 24, 1943.
    151: *The New Yorker*, May 27, 1939.
    152: *The New Yorker*, December 23, 1939.
    156: *The New Yorker*, June 15, 1935.
    157: Ad for Heinz soups, *The New Yorker*, April 7, 1934.
    160: Illustration for "If You Ask Me," *PM*, October 8, 1940.
    163: *The New Yorker*, November 30, 1935.
    164: *People Today*, October 21, 1953.
    165: *The New Yorker*, April 17, 1937.
    166: Unpublished letter.
    169: *The New Yorker*, May 17, 1941.

Writings

"Men, Women, and Dogs," *The New Yorker*, April 17, 1937.
"I Like Dogs," *For Men*, April 1939.
"Dogs I have Scratched," *Harper's Bazaar*, January 1933.
"Why Not Die?" *The New Yorker*, September 21, 1935.
"An Author Stands Corrected," *The New Yorker*, October 12, 1935.
"My Day (With Apologies to Eleanor Roosevelt)," *The New Yorker*, February 15, 1936.

"The Uprising of the Animals and Other Observations of the Natural World"
        "Letter from the States," *Bermudian*, February 1950;
        "If You Ask Me," *PM*, October 10, 1944;
        "If You Ask Me," *PM*, February 24, 1941;
        "Letter from the States," *Bermudian*, May 1950.

"A Letter from Roger," *The New Yorker*, November 12, 1932.

"I Break Everything I Touch," *The Man*, 1941.

"More Ice Added to U.S. As Thousands Cheer," *The New Yorker*, December 22, 1934.

"An Outline of the Byrd Report," *The New Yorker*, July 26, 1930.

"Thoughts from Mr. Tierney," *The New Yorker*, February 13, 1932.

"Polo in the Home," *The New Yorker*, September 17, 1927.

"No Sex after the First of the Year," Chicago *Tribune*, December 7, 1929.

"The Story of the Bicycle," *Bermudian*, May 1940.

"Help! Help! Another Classificationization," unpublished, March 30, 1956.

"Look Out for the Warelians!" *The New Yorker*, April 1, 1939.

"Brief Biography," from an article, "Freud: or the Future of Psychoanalysis," in *Whither, Whither, or After Sex, What?: A Symposium to End all Symposiums*, edited by Walter S. Hankel, New York: Macaulay, 1930.

ℬRIEF BIOGRAPHY

James Thurber was born in the blowy uplands of Columbus, Ohio, in a district known as "the Flats," which, for half of the year, was partially underwater and during the rest of the time was an outcropping of live granite, rising in dry weather to a height of two hundred feet. This condition led to moroseness, skepticism, jumping when shots were fired, membership in a silver cornet band, and, finally, a system of floating pulley-baskets by means of which the Thurber family was raised up to and lowered down from the second floor of the old family homestead. Psychoanalysis, first as a possible way out and then (since this failed) as an academic study, absorbed James's attention. His brothers, William and Robert, went in for athletics and found a way out in that direction. James, however, used the floating pulley-baskets until such great crowds of sightseers were attracted that he left in an old 1903 High Dudgeon for New York. He settled first in West Eleventh Street and then in West Eleventh Street—three doors farther east than the first, or old, West Eleventh Street place.

During the war James Thurber was nowhere to be found and was sometimes mistaken for Ambrose Bierce. He turned up, finally, on the Soissons front nineteen days after the Armistice and was invalided back to Paris by a Y.M.C.A. worker and a French Colonial sentinel, who found him bravely holding, single-handed, a small tin bar, or bistro, not far from the Chemin des Dames. He had lost his overshoes and muffler and had had to throw away most of the souvenirs he had collected, because of difficulty in climbing out of abandoned trenches with them. In Paris he rejoined the staff of the American Embassy, which had been wondering where he was, but shortly thereafter he was reprimanded in action, and invalided back to America. Psychoanalysis again failed as a cure and he pursued it once more as a study—with results which we all know, in a hazy sort of way. Today, he is invalided in and out of the *New Yorker* office.

[—James Thurber]